The Scientific Truth of the Golf Swing

Improve your golf game with a scientific approach

by Steen Winther, M.Sc.

WWW.THINKINGOLFER.COM

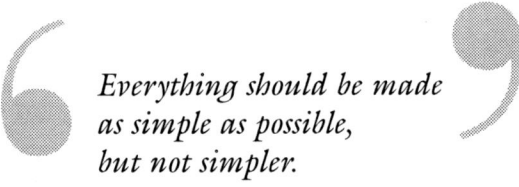

Everything should be made as simple as possible, but not simpler.

– Albert Einstein

Copyright © 2006 Steen Winther, All rights reserved.
This edition: Version 1.1
ISBN-10 1-4116-9717-0
ISBN-13 978-1-4116-9717-1

Layout & illustrations: Visual Clarity, NSW Australia, www.visualclarity.com.au

Introduction	3
Chapter 1 **Knowledge** is the key	5
Chapter 2 What is a **good golf swing?**	9
Chapter 3 **Club** meets **ball**	13
Chapter 4 Club **design parameters**	20
Chapter 5 **Ball flight** and aerodynamics	33
Chapter 6 May the **force** be with you	41
Chapter 7 **Notations & definitions**	47
Chapter 8 Practical guide – **The set-up**	53
Chapter 9 Practical guide – **The swing**	61
Chapter 10 Golf swing **myths**	77
Chapter 11 **Anatomy** of the golf swing	87
Index	91

Golf is a science, the study of a lifetime, in which you may exhaust yourself but never your subject.

– David R. Forgan

It is evident that the act of swinging a golf club optimally is very difficult. If it was easy, most golf swings would look identical. And, they would provide identical results – which they certainly do not. There are, however, similarities to be found in good swings. Hidden behind all sorts of mannerisms – obscured by our obsession with the flight of the ball rather than the swing – lies fundamental truths, founded on the nature of golf equipment, course conditions, laws of physics, and our bio-mechanical features. Many of these fundamentals are revealed in the British study from 1972, "Search for the Perfect Golf Swing," which still constitutes a formidable guide of reference to almost any subject within the game of golf. My study goes into further detail with the swing itself – explaining HOW the golfer should use his body to produce a fundamentally sound swing and WHY these recommendations are scientifically sound.

Before we proceed, I have to make apologies to both female readers and left-handed golfers: I have chosen to speak of the golfer as "he" in this study simply because it facilitates my writing. Furthermore, I have chosen only to describe a right-handed golfer's universe. This is because the golf swing for the left-hander is an absolute mirror image of a right-handed swing, so every instruction is valid as long as the reader substitutes left for right and associates a clockwise rotation with "opening" and counter-clockwise with "closing."

Please note, however that all golfers should be aware of the difference of perception between left- and right-handed swings. We are so accustomed to watching right-handed swings, that to most of us a left-handed swing looks wrong, even though it is a mirror image of a familiar right-handed swing.

My background is first and foremost an on-going love/hate relationship with the game, now spanning more than 20 years. Being endowed with fairly modest athletically skills, I have had to grind a golf swing out of the dust at the practice ground, the good old-fashioned way. A scientific education, Master of Science in mechanical engineering, and a very keen "how does it work" mentality has enabled me to finally approach the nirvana of golf: A total understanding of the golf swing – or, at least, of the fundamental elements found in all good swings.

Through this study I hope to help you in your quest for a better understanding of golf and, thus, a happier golf life.

Best regards,
Steen Winther,
www.thinkingolfer.com

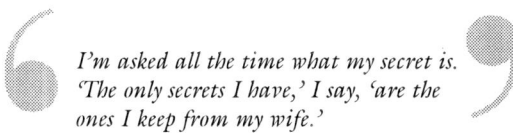

I'm asked all the time what my secret is. 'The only secrets I have,' I say, 'are the ones I keep from my wife.'

– Bob Toski

Chapter 1

Knowledge is the key

The swing of a good amateur or professional golfer holds quite a few secrets – some of which are often not even known to the owner of the swing. This is a logical deduction from the fact that it is very easy to find conflicting statements about the foundations of the swing – even from the games most prominent players.

Misinformation is **abundant**

One world-beater states that he uses his right hand to "whip the club through at impact," whereas another uses his legs as the "primary source for power." Obviously they can't both be correct as not even the most well trained right hand has anywhere near the strength as a pair of legs. But even though the professionals do not agree on how a

CHAPTER 1 | THE SCIENTIFIC TRUTH OF THE GOLF SWING

golf swing should be executed, they somehow manage to play the game well enough to earn a living. And, often, a very good living that is indeed.

You **can't trust** the gifted players

The problem with learning golf from good players is that they don't need to know what they are doing – they "just do it," to use Nike's expression. Most of them learned the game at a young age and it has become second nature. But the fact remains that if you ask them what they do and why they do it that way, you do not get consistent replies – they simply don't know!

Learning golf reminds me very much of learning mathematics: Some people get it very easily, but most don't. And, the gifted ones have great difficulty understanding why the not so gifted ones can't learn. When you're gifted, it's a piece of cake – you don't even have to think – the solutions are instinctively clear. One unfortunate consequence of being gifted is that you'll probably end up writing the text books for future students, which only widens the gap between teacher and pupil, but that's an entirely different discussion.

The **missing link** of golf

In my opinion, every fit person of average constitution is able to develop a good swing and play the game to a low handicap. The only provision is that you play the game with emphasis on scoring and have adequate perception of what you're trying to accomplish. This insight into the mechanics of the golf swing – liberated of hearsay and myths – is truly the missing link of golf for golfers that are not naturally gifted.

Information **galore**

Recent years have seen an enormous growth in the available amount of instructional materials about golf. The traditional media, books, and magazines have been supplemented with new media like instruction conveyed via videotape, DVD, specialised golf television (e.g. "The Golf Channel"), and the Internet. There exists a great number of interactive websites where a player can submit his swing (on video) for analysis or get information on how to swing the club optimally based on kinematic analysis of the best tour pros' swings. Only a small fraction of this wealth of information is brilliant – most is trash in form of scams that promise much and deliver little. The problem, of course, is how to distinguish between what works and what doesn't.

The large dynamic forces are what makes the golf swing so difficult to master – even if you know what you would like to change and are using a video camera to guide the process. A swing that feels very different (and uncomfortable) after a swing change, often appears unaltered on video. And, on top of this, you have lost the repeatability of the original swing. So, mimicking a model golfer doesn't really work – it's like looking for a needle in a haystack. The only way to force the club and your body into new positions is to swing correctly – to use the proper muscles in a proper fashion. This has the result of changing your swing positions and your ball striking.

It is, in fact, possible for a golfer to change very serious mechanical swing flaws during one single practice session. But the swing problems have to be identified in advance and the necessary changes planned from a sound knowledge of swing mechanics.

CHAPTER 1 | THE SCIENTIFIC TRUTH OF THE GOLF SWING

The purpose of this guide is not to put the finishing touches on an almost perfect swing, but to teach the fundamentals of the effortless, powerful swing that can be adopted by everyone. Great is the number of world-class players who have sported all sorts of smaller or larger deviations from simplicity in their swings – but these players all possess sound fundamentals. Their individual mannerisms may or may not be the reason for their success in the game, but they are definitely not required to hit good shots and shouldn't be imitated. An experienced player typically tweaks elements in his grip, stance, and swing in order to obtain greater repeatability and precision. These individual traits can't be taught but must be invented – if required – by the player in his search for ever lower scores.

Golf **nirvana** is in sight

To feel a fundamentally sound golf swing, is a wonderful and life-changing experience. You swing easy but hit longer and straighter than ever before. Your error rate drops dramatically and your feel increases. The pieces of the puzzle begin to fit together. If you reach golf nirvana, a holistic understanding of the game, you'll be able to distinguish good golf advice from poor golf advice. You'll realize that many established teachers, players, and writers have a flawed understanding of the swing, and that they teach methods founded on wrong assumptions.

Let's go and explore what this crazy old game is really all about...

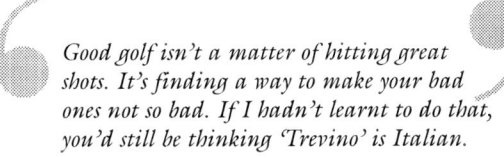

Good golf isn't a matter of hitting great shots. It's finding a way to make your bad ones not so bad. If I hadn't learnt to do that, you'd still be thinking 'Trevino' is Italian.

– Lee Trevino

Chapter 2

What is a **good** golf swing?

A good golf swing is first and foremost a repeatable action that provides predictable results. It is not necessary to be particularly strong or long of the tee to play good golf and, by "good golf," I refer to low scoring. On golf courses around the world you'll find plenty of amateur golfers who hit truly outstanding shots during a round, but also a lot of not-so-great shots. They go for broke on every shot and, as a consequence, make a lot of birdies and a lot of "others." This, I suppose, can be fun, but it is definitely not the way to improve your scoring. Consistency is the name of the game.

Scramble for birdies

The value of consistency is proven in the "scramble" match form, where a team of golfers all hit their shots from the same spot, always selecting to play their next shots from where the best placed ball landed. This virtually eliminates mistakes and a team of four golfers with mid-handicaps, say 12-24, are able to play most courses under par, notwithstanding that none of them could get anywhere near this number in ordinary play on their own.

Golf is a **serial game**

The reason that it is of vital importance to minimise errors, is that golf, to a great extent, is a serial game: Every shot you play on a hole, except the put that drops into the hole, sets up the next shot. So, a good drive means an easier, shorter second shot from a good lie in the fairway, which again sets up a shorter put or third shot with greater chance for success. This is why we see those unbelievably hot streaks, where a player makes a whole string of birdies.

Unfortunately, the principle also holds true for bad shots and with even greater consequences: A short or errand drive sets up a more difficult scenario with less chance of success. Just one bad swing or poor decision can ruin your chances of a good score on a hole. For example: No miraculous shot can save the score for a player who has hit OB (out of bounds). The stroke and distance penalty **can never be overcome**! This is why it is preferable to play safe when you are in trouble, accepting your penalty and minimising the damage instead of attempting a miraculous shot to make up for the error.

You often hear TV commentators remark that a player has "regained a dropped shot" with a birdie. But, like so much from the idiot box, that is nonsense. Because the player would be still better off if he hadn't made the bogey in the first place. Good shots breed good shots. Bad shots breed bad shots (and high scores).

The player who hits a lot of mediocre shots that stay out of trouble, plus a few good ones, easily ties he who hits a lot of brilliant shots interspersed with a few disastrous ones.

The playing **professionals**

To be a successful playing pro, it is mandatory that you hit the ball straight and long, so that you comfortably can reach all par-4s in regulation, and many of the par-5s. These high demands are brought on by the fierce level of competition. Every week there seems to arrive a new kid on tour, who hits the ball a mile, and has sharp short game and a beautiful putting stroke. You simply cannot have any major weaknesses if you are to make a living on the pro circuits. The game is too difficult when you have to get up and down for par while your fellow players are putting for birdies. That being said, please also note that the incredibly low scores shot every week on the professional tours, are produced by players in form. A lot of other excellent players did not perform well enough to make the cut, and some of those who did only produced mediocre rounds (in the mid to high seventies) during the weekend. This just goes to show how difficult the game is, even for the best players.

A **ballet** of man and club

Watching a professional or even good amateur golfer hitting balls is a great joy to any keen golfer. They make the act look so easy and effortless. It's a ballet of man and club, the same movements repeated over and over – every swing of the club resulting in identical ball flights as if every ball followed the same invisible path in the sky. Yet, it is also an act of magic because, as every aspiring golfer knows, it is far from easy to reach such a high level of performance.

The **learning** process

If you start playing the game as a child, several factors work in your favor at mastering the swing: You probably learn by imitating good players. This ability diminishes with age, possibly because grownups tend to act through formalized learning rather than intuition. We are control freaks. Another major factor helping a child honing a good swing is the lack of physical strength – the child cannot overpower the club, he has to swing it. In contrast, most adults have overdeveloped upper bodies. Think about it, most daily tasks involve only arms and hands (and our butt). As a consequence, we also tend to overemphasise the role of hands & arms when swinging a golf club.

But not all naturally gifted kids grow up to become good golfers; the reason being, that there is much more to the game than "merely" hitting good shots. Golfing lore is flooded with misinformation and myths that easily confuse players to a degree that it hinders their ability to obtaining their true potential.

Let us therefore get some facts on the table about what happens when the club strikes the ball. Only when you have a crystal clear picture of what you are trying to achieve should you direct your attention to the swing itself.

In the actual playing of the game, the golfer cannot keep a great amount of theory in mind and have any attention left to bestow upon the ball.

– John Dunn

Chapter 3

Club meets ball

For the golfer to have a precise idea of how he wants the club to strike the ball – the objective of the swing, so to speak – he must understand what happens in the interaction between club and ball at the moment of impact.

Precision required

The one factor that facilitates the striking of the golf ball is that it is immobile. This, of course, makes it very much easier to hit than if it moved, but it's still not easy to hit flush. One obvious reason is that the margin for error is small. Even today's oversized equipment doesn't allow for a large margin of error before the consequences for the shot are dire.

CHAPTER 3 | THE SCIENTIFIC TRUTH OF THE GOLF SWING

The largest margin for error applies for shots hit toward the heel or the toe of the club. Depending on the design of the club, the deviation of the impact point from the middle of the clubface can be up to an inch (25 mm) before having a major detrimental effect on the shot.

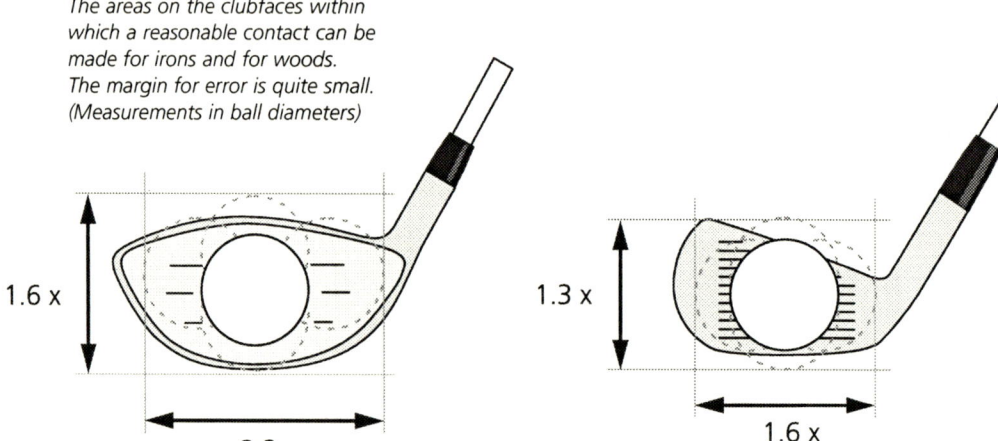

The areas on the clubfaces within which a reasonable contact can be made for irons and for woods. The margin for error is quite small. (Measurements in ball diameters)

The tolerances in the lateral plane are much tighter. Not only do you need to limit the strike to a small area on the clubface, but there is the additional risk of hitting "the big ball," the Earth. If the clubface digs into the ground a fraction of an inch before striking the ball (a heavy hit), the strike suffers because turf and dirt comes between clubface and ball. If, on the other hand, the clubhead is hovering above the ground at the point of impact, (doesn't get to the bottom of the ball), the ball is hit "thin" and the strike does not transfer all the energy of the clubhead to the ball.

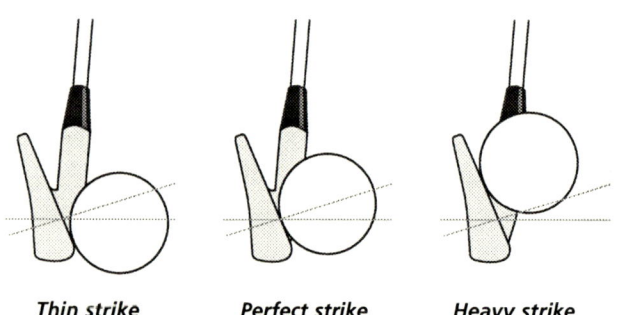

Thin strike   **Perfect strike**   **Heavy strike**

CLUB MEETS BALL | CHAPTER 3

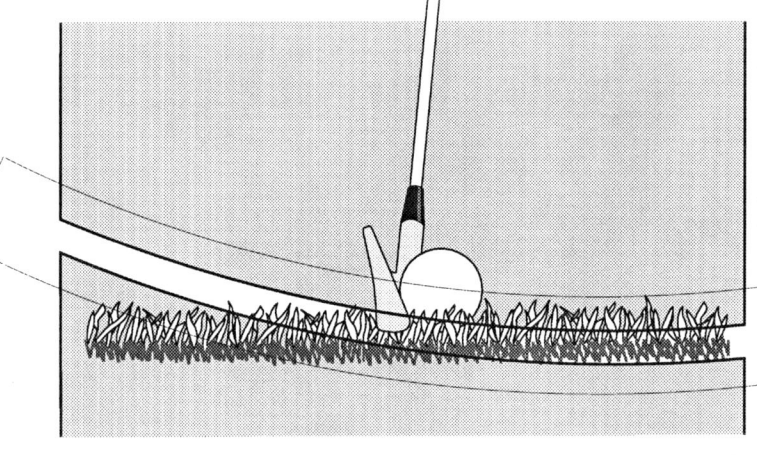

This narrow "tunnel" separates a good shot from a topped shot or heavy shot when hitting from turf. The tolerance within which a strike is solid is only about half an inch (12 mm).

If the clubhead is further above ground than the radius of the ball (0.84 inch, 21 mm), the shot is "topped;" it won't have any backspin at all and just rolls along the ground. So a very precise strike is needed. If you get the chance to inspect the clubs of an expert player, you should find a spot the size of a small coin on every clubface where the plating has been worn – indicating that these are indeed the tools of a master craftsman.

Because the ball rests on the ground, all golfers tower over it forcing them to swing the club up and away in the backswing, and down to and through the ball in the forward swing. The path of the clubhead describes some sort of inclined, elongated circle with a low point at the ball or a few inches past the ball. This is what is commonly referred to as "hitting down on the ball." In the latter case a divot is taken from the turf. It is essential to realize, that divot-taking is a result of the set-up to the ball – it does not require any finely timed use of the hands or "dip" in the knees. On the contrary – you use exactly the same swing as for any other shot, the clubhead just happens to contact the turf after the ball is hit. If you try to take divots deliberately, you'll end up digging trenches in no time.

15

CHAPTER 3 | THE SCIENTIFIC TRUTH OF THE GOLF SWING

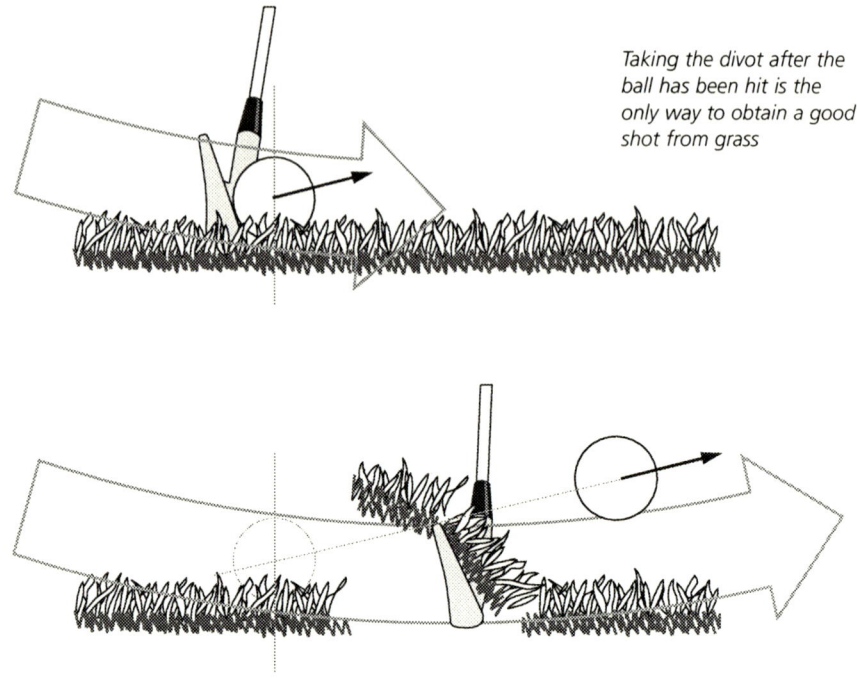

Taking the divot after the ball has been hit is the only way to obtain a good shot from grass

In a good swing, the club approaches the ball at a relatively steep angle, thus minimizing the amount of grass that the club has to travel through prior to the strike. The hands always lead the clubhead into the shot, in other words, they are in front of a vertical line through the ball.

It is simply impossible to hit the ball in the downswing and take a turf if the clubhead overtakes the hands before impact. This is called "scooping" and the only usable application is when hitting an extra high shot from a tee-peg. In his books, Ben Hogan refers to how good players do the exact opposite; they de-loft their irons at impact for a low, penetrating ball flight, compared to the less talented players' much higher and weaker flighted shots.

When the ball is buried in high grass, it is best played with the hands up to a foot (30 cm) or so in front of the ball. This has the effect of de-lofting the club, forcing the player to take a lofted club to make sure that the ball doesn't get caught in the grass.

CLUB MEETS BALL | CHAPTER 3

Usually, you don't want to make contact with the ground before the ball is hit. Exceptions include explosion shots from bunkers and fairway wood shots from very bad lies where you can obtain a reasonable ball contact by hitting the ground an inch or two before the ball. The flat sole of the fairway wood skates along the ground bouncing off the surface whereas a similar shot with an iron results in total failure. This is the reason that some rescue clubs have longitudinal rails in the sole, helping to square the clubface when ploughing through the turf prior to impact.

Impact

When the club strikes the ball, energy is transferred from club to ball. A typical hit takes only around 1/2000th of a second, but during this short time the ball accelerates to a velocity far greater than that of the club and the club loses speed due to the exchange of energy. The ball is compressed like a spring and jumps away with 40-50 percent greater velocity than that of the club before impact. Correspondingly, the club looses around 30 percent of its speed.

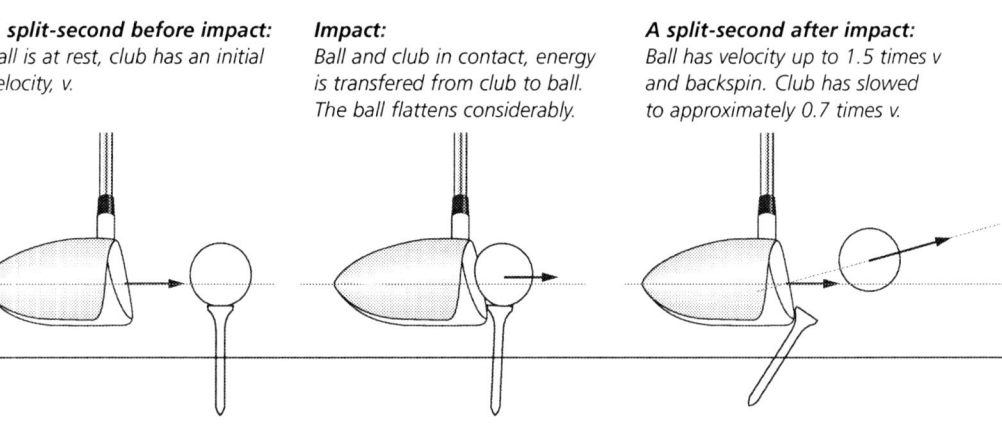

A split-second before impact: Ball is at rest, club has an initial velocity, v.

Impact: Ball and club in contact, energy is transfered from club to ball. The ball flattens considerably.

A split-second after impact: Ball has velocity up to 1.5 times v and backspin. Club has slowed to approximately 0.7 times v.

17

CHAPTER 3 | THE SCIENTIFIC TRUTH OF THE GOLF SWING

The average force of impact between club and ball is huge, 6000-8000 N (Newtons), which corresponds to a weight of 600-800 kg. Impact is, therefore, definitely a hit and the large force is produced by the sudden deceleration of the clubhead – not by muscular action. In other words, what you do with your hands during the half millisecond of impact doesn't matter. The most interesting consequence of this realization is that only the mass of the clubhead interacts with the ball – the mass of the shaft, grip, and players' hands and arms are irrevelent.

The "accelerate through the ball" **myth**

Provided that the ball is hit solidly, the clubhead speed is the only parameter that determines the ball speed (for a given club) and, consequently, how far the shot flies. A club travelling at 100 mph (44 m/s) – driver speed for a good amateur – only travels approximately .86 inches (24 mm) during impact, close to half a ball diameter. The ball doesn't register any acceleration other than that caused by the large force of impact, so the advice that you need to accelerate the club through impact is quite unfounded and wrong. And, this goes for every club in the bag, including the putter. But as a swing thought or mantra, "accelerate through the ball" can be valuable, because it prevents the golfer from quitting on the shot. It just isn't correctly phrased or understood by the majority of golfers.

Speeding Rules **Enforced**

Nowadays, manufacturers can produce golf balls that are capable of rebounding after impact at a far greater speed than traditional golf balls. This is because modern golf balls are solid, made of synthetic rubber and plastics, where traditional balls are wound of hundreds of yards of rubber string enclosed by a solid shell. But such "lively" balls are not allowed under the rules of the governing bodies of golf. The Royal and Ancient Golf Club of St. Andrews (R&A) and the United States Golf Association (USGA) place very strict limits on the initial velocity of a golf ball struck under fixed conditions. So, in order for the manufacturers to design legal golf balls that travel further, they have to come up with better aerodynamics – new dimple patterns and materials that optimise the trade-off between spin and carry for a given clubhead speed. This is a sound reason for producing a whole range of balls, each optimised for a different clubhead speed and ball trajectory.

When I started playing golf in 1982, most club golfers played hard-covered balls with solid rubber cores for maximum distance. The better players used wound balls with hard covers or wound balls with soft covers – allegedly for improved feel and spin in short shots. The trade-off for using soft-covered balls, typically made from balata, was a very noticable loss of distance. Very few top professionals would play a hard-covered ball in competition, although Christy O'Connor Sr. swore by his Top-Flite and Lee Trevino hit it big with Strata.

Today, all balls are solid rubber with a variety of covers, but the soft-covered balls travel just as far as the hard-covered balls; so, everybody enjoys the length of the old "cannonballs." This, I believe, is the major reason for the huge increse in driving distance for the top players.

COR = coefficient of restitution

COR is a generel term from physics that describes the "springiness" of a collision. A COR of 1 corresponds to a perfectly elastic impact where all energy is preserved. A COR less than 1 indicates that some energy is lost during impact as heat, permanent deformations, etc. – which is unavoidable in the real world.

In golf, COR has until recently been used to denote the "springiness" of clubfaces, or the spring-like effect. The club gives in to the force of impact and, like the ball, sports an ability to store and release energy during the hit. The clubface acts similar to a trampoline, giving the ball a higher velocity than if hit by a solid clubhead. The effect is most pronounced in metal woods, where manufactures obtain high values by thinning clubfaces. Consequently, this parameter is also under the control by the ruling bodies, but there is a lot of debate regarding the allowable size and how it should be measured. The latest "official apparatus" measures the rebound time of a steel pendulum hitting the clubface rather peacefully. This instrument gives ratings of impact duration, called Characteristic Time (CT) as is measured in microseconds. The "old" notation is a COR value of a ball hitting the clubface. After 2008 the largest allowable COR will be .83, which allegedly is equivalent to a CT of 257 microseconds.

It is interesting that the governing bodies operate with very technical and artificial terms instead of focusing on what happens when a real club hits a real ball; that is, examining $COR_{Club+Ball}$ and the resulting ball flight. One thing is certain, if you can't hit the centre of the clubface, the effect is rendered useless, like jumping on the edge of a trampoline. There is no spring-like effect.

Loft

Every golf club excluding some putters has loft. Loft is the inclination of the clubface from vertical. Most putters have a few degrees of loft, common drivers anywhere from 7.5-12 degrees (with some as low as 4 degrees), fairway woods 13-28 degrees, and irons 17-64 degrees. The loft of the club is responsible for two major effects: Firstly, as the name implies, it gives loft to the ball making it leave the clubface at a higher angle than the club's angle of attack (or it's velocity vector); secondly, it imparts backspin on the ball. Some of the clubhead energy is transformed to forward motion and some to ball rotation. The more loft on the clubface, the more backspin, but also correspondingly less forward velocity. This is the main reason why clubs with a lot of loft hit considerably shorter than stronger lofted clubs. The length of the shaft is negligible in this context. Here you also find the explanation for why the dreadful topped sand iron shot travels up to three times further than intended. It flies like a drive.

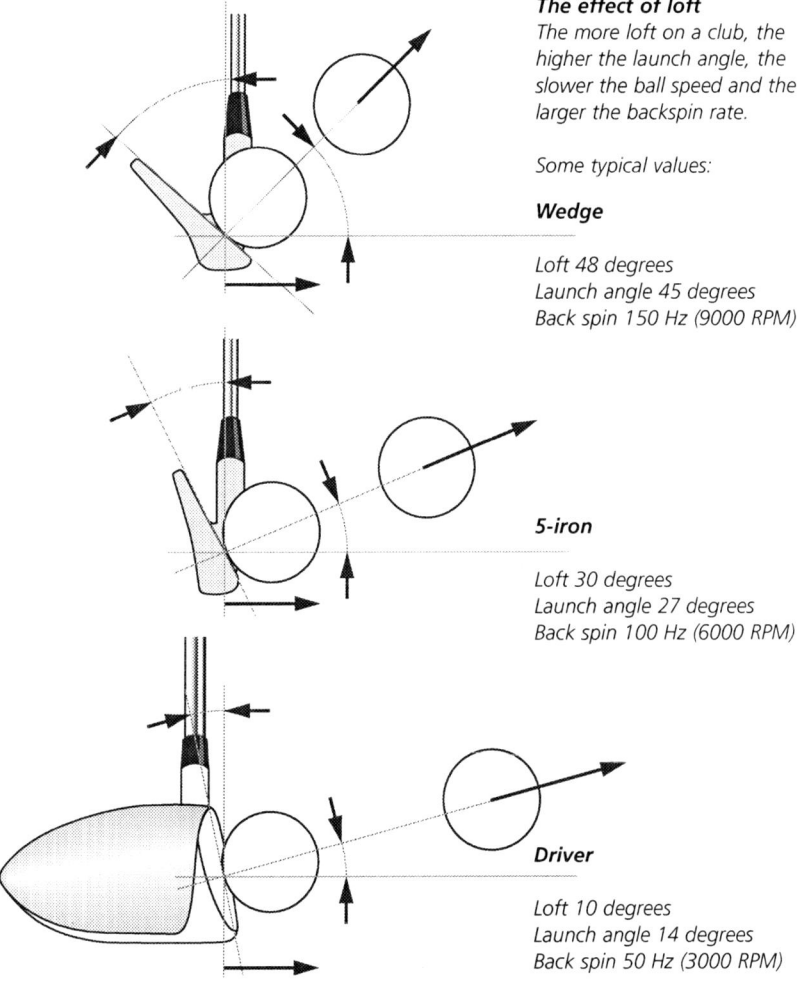

The effect of loft
The more loft on a club, the higher the launch angle, the slower the ball speed and the larger the backspin rate.

Some typical values:

Wedge

*Loft 48 degrees
Launch angle 45 degrees
Back spin 150 Hz (9000 RPM)*

5-iron

*Loft 30 degrees
Launch angle 27 degrees
Back spin 100 Hz (6000 RPM)*

Driver

*Loft 10 degrees
Launch angle 14 degrees
Back spin 50 Hz (3000 RPM)*

Effective loft

At impact, the ball registers the angle of attack, the precision of attack (where on the clubface impact takes place), the clubhead speed, and the effective loft of the club. That is all. I speak of effective loft because the loft that the ball experiences depends on all of the above mentioned parameters. It is very common for golfers to hit the ball with either the heel or the toe of the club off the ground. The reason can be a poor setup, a poor swing or that the equipment is improperly fitted to the golfer; for example have too short or too soft shafts or faulty lie angles.

Before I had my own clubs properly fitted, I hit all my irons with the heel of the clubs well off the ground. This would normally result in faded or sliced shots, but I always played with a draw, so I unknowingly compensated for the open clubface by letting the clubhead pass my hands at impact, thus closing the face. With the clubhead in this position, it is almost impossible to get a good contact from tight lies because the toe tends to dig into the turf. My quest for a good swing would probably have been significantly easier had I been club fitted much earlier.

Making use of a high-speed video camera and golf analysis software for the computer is a good way of checking if your lie angles or shaft lengths are off. You can measure the change in shaft angles from address through impact and, at the same time, determinate if a problem lies in the equipment or with the swing.

The flyer

A flyer is a shot out of relatively high grass, where the grass comes between the clubface and the ball, thereby changing the friction and the characteristics of the strike. Generally, the amount of backspin is reduced and the initial velocity probably increases. The resultant shot will travel lower and longer, and takes longer to stop. The "opposite" shot of a flyer is the fairway bunker shot, where a very small amount of sand comes between the ball and the clubface – a few grains of sand on the ball at the strike can do the trick. Here the amount of friction is seriously increased and the ball travels shorter than expected, and stops very fast – often spinning violently backwards or sideways when it hits the green.

Clubhead mass

Studies of the initial velocity of the ball versus clubhead mass shows that the mass of the clubhead is of minor importance compared to the speed at which the club is travelling at impact. In other words, swinging a very heavy club doesn't produce a much longer shot. But, a heavy club requires a sound swing to be swung with high velocity. You can't get away with last minute adjustments by the hands and arms or being out of balance when using a heavy club. Therefore, the trend is to make clubs very light using high tech materials like carbon fibres and titanium, giving even untrained amateurs the best chance of obtaining high clubhead speed. A light club, on the other hand, provides less information (feedback) to the player's hands because of the smaller forces involved. Thus, it is beneficial to use heavier clubs for additional feel when pitching and chipping.

clubhead mass	ball speed / clubhead speed
150 g	1.39
200 g	1.47
250 g	1.53
500 g	1,67
1000 g	1.75
∞	1.83

Typical values for the correlation between ball and clubhead speed for different clubhead masses. A driver head weighs 200-250 g.

CHAPTER 3 | THE SCIENTIFIC TRUTH OF THE GOLF SWING

Backspin – you've got it whether you like it or not

All golf clubs impart backspin on the ball and help it into the air – they have positive lofts. There is no such thing as a good golf shot hit with topspin. This is purely the concoction of a vivid imagination. As there are no clubs with negative loft, the only way to impart topspin on a golf ball is to hit it with the leading edge of the club above its equator. The resulting shot is the worm-killer with which newcomers to the game are all to familiar. Even if the shot is hit very much on the upswing from a high tee, the resulting flight is a fast diving ball with negative lift. Hovever, there certainly is a benefit to be had in finding the optimum combination of launch angle and spin, as many golfers tend to hit weak flighted drives with too much spin. In other words, they tend to propel the ball upward rather than forward.

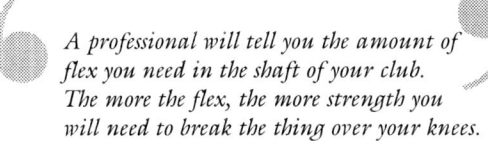

A professional will tell you the amount of flex you need in the shaft of your club. The more the flex, the more strength you will need to break the thing over your knees.

– Stephen Baker

Chapter 4

Club **design** parameters

The shape of the clubhead has a pronounced effect on shots that are not hit out of the sweet spot of the club. In other words, if golfers always hit every single shot out of the sweet spot, the clubs could be designed totally different than they are today. But as it is, club manufactures seek to make modern clubs immune to poor striking, as long as the golfer makes contact with some part of the clubface.

The **sweet** spot

The sweet spot is the point of contact on the clubface that lies in line with the club's centre of mass. When the club makes impact with the ball in the sweet spot, maximum energy is transferred to the ball and a minimum of torque twists the club. The strike feels effortless, perfect.

CHAPTER 4 | THE SCIENTIFIC TRUTH OF THE GOLF SWING

It's that famed sensation golfers rave about. You feel the club being decelerated rapidly by the impact, but without any uncomfortable feedback in the hands. You can experience a similar feeling in the old Henry Cotton tire-drill, by swinging an iron (at full speed) into the thread of a car tire lying on the ground.

Mishits

When the golfer makes a less than perfect strike, the effects are severe in a number of ways. The ball obtains neither its maximum velocity nor its expected spin rate, as some energy is lost. Most of it is transformed into a torque that twists the clubhead, this is the very opposite of a perfect strike, and the golfer feels the grip twisting his hands. The severity depends on the degree of off-center contact, the clubhead speed, the forgiveness of the club, and the characteristics of the shaft. A bad miss in the toe with a long iron can rip open the skin of the hand, a pretty painful and unpleasant experience.

Game improving clubs

Club manufactures can make their clubs more immune to off-center hits by increasing their moment of inertia. Karsten Solheim, a clever engineer with a passion for golf, revolutionized the golf equipment industry and founded a multi-million dollar business by designing clubs with designs based on physics rather than tradition and aesthetics. He introduced the first perimeter weighed iron clubs, in addition to the putters whose unusual sound when striking the ball gave name to the company, PING.

Moment of **inertia**

Moment of inertia (MOI) is a physics term that describes an object's resistance to being rotated. It is analogous to mass, that describes the object's resistance to being moved. The object's mass contributes to its moment of inertia, but what really matters is how the mass is distributed. The nearer to the centre of mass, the lower the moment of inertia; the farther from the centre of mass, the higher the moment of inertia. Or, in slightly less scientific terms, the more compact the clubhead, the less its moment of inertia.

You witness the concept of MOI at work in a tightrope walker using a balancing pole. A short dumbbell would be of no benefit, but with the mass placed at the ends of a long pole, its MOI becomes huge and the tightrope walker is actually able to lean on the pole for support.

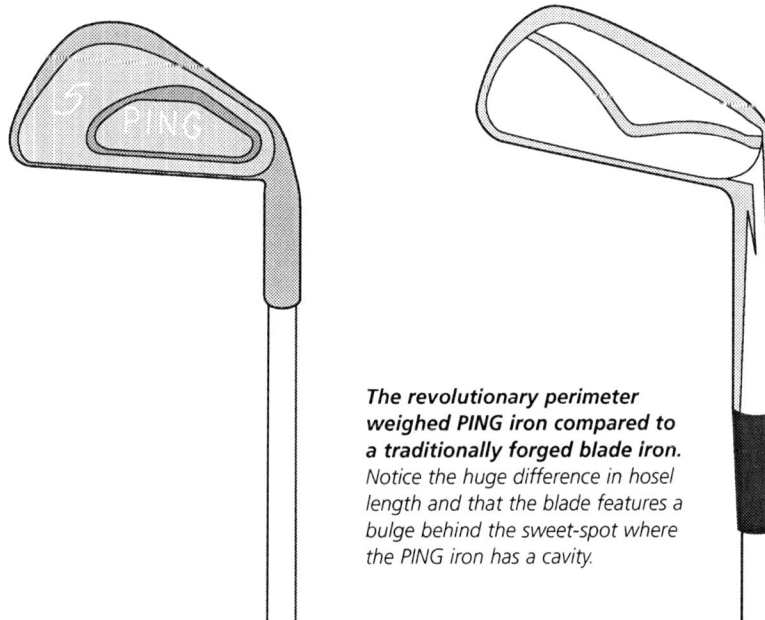

The revolutionary perimeter weighed PING iron compared to a traditionally forged blade iron. Notice the huge difference in hosel length and that the blade features a bulge behind the sweet-spot where the PING iron has a cavity.

When evaluating clubs, we are primarily interested in two separate MOIs, that of the clubhead around its centre of gravity and that of the whole club felt by the golfer when swinging, related, but not identical to swing-weight.

Swing-weight

Swing-weight is an arbitrary measure for a club's balance and mass. In physical terms, it is *the torque of the club's weight from a point 12 inches (30.5 cm) from the top of the grip* measured in ounce-inches. In other words, it is the mass of the club (in ounces) multiplied with the distance from the top end to the centre of gravity, less 12 inches. You can either use a fancy apparatus (if you are a clubfitter or keen on gadgets) or an ordinary kitchen scale and a ruler to find a club's swing-weight. It's a simple procedure, but you must convert the torque value in ounce-inches to its so called lorythmic counterpart to obtain the well known alphanumeric code the manufacturers use.

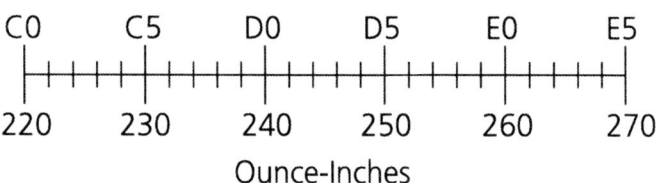

Lorythmic swing-weight scale

A high swing-weight (D9, E0 etc.) means that the club feels heavy to the golfer; a low swing-weight (C7, C8 etc.) means that it feels light. But swing-weight is, contrary to the name, not a measure for how heavy a club feels when it is swung. It is a static measurement and, when contemplating the feel of a golf club, dead weight, MOI and shaft flex all have huge influences. You can assure yourself of this by going through the racks of clubs in a well-stocked golf shop. Many clubs labeled with identical swing-weights actually feel vastly different. This is certainly one of the areas in the golf manufacturing industry where the current terms are far from adequate in giving a satisfactory description of the equipment. Until a more precise nomenclature is invented, taking into account shaft stiffness and mass distribution, there is no substitute for trial and error in selecting the tools of the trade.

Perimeter weighing

By placing a lot of material of the iron head around the perimeter of the clubface, the moment of inertia is increased and off-center hits are somewhat compensated. This is the so-called perimeter weighing that is a feature in most iron clubs nowadays.

Actually, the concept of large moments of inertia is nothing new to golf. Every old fashioned wooden club possesses quite a large moment of inertia, because the centre of gravity lies far behind the clubface. For a shot hit off-center, this is analogous to having concentrations of mass in the toe and heel of the club. In addition, wooden clubs would have metal sole-plates lowering the centre of gravity, thus providing higher shots, and often an extra (brass) weight at the very rear of the club, enhancing the weight behind the sweet spot and further increasing the moment of inertia.

Another design element, found in older wooden clubs, is "bulge," a convex face curvature of the entire clubface. In combination with the large moment of inertia this helps control the sidespin of the ball through the gear-effect. With the almost universal elimination of clubs made of wood since the 1990s, the gear-effect seems to have fallen out of favor, as you find a lot of "metal woods" [fairway metals and metal drivers] that have little or no face curvature. But most have retained the classic lines of the wooden clubs, big round heads, and, due to the extreme peripheral placement of the mass and their huge sizes, they have far better resistance to off-center hits (larger MOI) than their predecessors.

Shaft **stiffness** and torque resistance

The role of the shaft in the golf club is much debated and often misunderstood. You hear the claim that the shaft adds speed to the clubhead because it loads (like a spring) in the backswing and unloads the energy in the downswing. This is one of the many thriving myths of golf. To get an idea of the amount of energy you can expect from the shaft, clamp the handle into a vice and pull back the clubhead. But please be careful. It is deceptively easy to bend or break a shaft. Even when you pull back the clubhead farther than safe for the shaft, the resistance is not very high; neither is the resultant speed of the clubhead when you let go of it. This effect does not add many yards to your drives, but it requirea a very strange and specific swing. The main problem is that the initial loading bends the shaft in the wrong direction! Consequently, shaft loading as a power reservoir is pure fiction, but is has a real effect of straining the shaft, and changing the position and orientation of the clubface during the swing.

Low mass is **more important** than stiffness

One reason that elderly and weak golfers are better off using softer shafts, is that softer shafts often are lighter than stiffer shafts. This allows them to be swung at greater speed without hitting harder. Weaker golfers can get away with using soft shafts because they don't have any use for stiffer shafts. The dynamic forces generated by low swing speed don't strain the shaft enough to put the swing geometry and striking precision in jeopardy.

Another reason for using a flexible shaft is that it allows the clubhead to flip through impact, even though the golfer is blocking the shot or not actively propelling the club forward. So, this is a rare example where shortcomings to the equipment outweighs the golfer's lack of skill and produces a better than expected result.

The **perfect** shaft

The perfect shaft would be without mass, infinitely stiff, and with infinite torsion stiffness. Every golfer from touring pro to duffer would use this shaft because it would enable the clubhead to be swung with the greatest speed and precision. In addition, it would provide excellent feedback to the hands regarding the position of the clubhead, having no interfering mass. In the real world, such a shaft cannot be made, so we have to settle for compromises. Stiffer shafts are heavier than comparable softer shafts and, thus, the golfer wastes energy swinging an object that doesn't contribute at all to the speed of the clubhead, because it doesn't exchange energy to the ball during the strike. But the stiff shaft does provide control and consistency to the shot. Also, the heavier the clubhead, the stiffer the shaft has to be to retain the club's playing characteristics.

Optical **illusions**

Note that the extreme shaft flex visible in some (mostly older) golf pictures – 10 inches plus – is an optical illusion caused by the camera's shutter design, which doesn't expose the whole negative instantaneous. The real life shaft flex is less than 2 inches (50 mm) in any direction for golfers with shafts that are well fitted to their swing.

CHAPTER 4 | THE SCIENTIFIC TRUTH OF THE GOLF SWING

Some of the **forces on the shaft**

1 A pull from the hands, mostly along the shaft, partly because of the circular motion, partly because the hands are accelerating.
   (Most notable at the change of direction between back- and downswing and just before impact.)

2 A bend in the heel-to-toe direction, and for wooden clubs also in the back-to-front direction because of centrifugal forces acting on clubhead.

3 Torsion during the downswing because the club is closing fast (Approx. 120 degrees in 0.3 second.)

4 At impact; torsion in case of off-center hit.

5 Wind drag from shaft and clubhead.

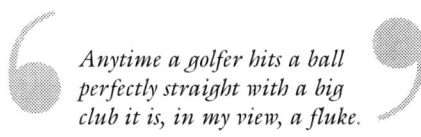

Anytime a golfer hits a ball perfectly straight with a big club it is, in my view, a fluke.

– Jack Nicklaus

Chapter 5

Ball flight and aerodynamics

When the ball leaves the clubface after being struck, it has an initial velocity, spin rate, and launch angle that determines the trajectory through the air and where the ball ends up. The dimples in the golf ball surface together with the spin gives the ball aerodynamic properties like those of an airplane wing. It is the Bernoulli effect that acts here: The upper half of the ball moves in the direction of the airflow past the ball, whereas the lower part moves against the flow. Thus, a local low pressure exists on top, a local high pressure at the bottom, and a resulting lift from the air is produced. The more spin the more lift. This is why you observe good shots climbing higher into the air than the initial launch angle suggested and why there is such focus on the design of improved dimple patterns. This is the only legitimate way of making a golf ball fly further without violating restrictions on size, weight, or coefficient of restitution.

CHAPTER 5 | THE SCIENTIFIC TRUTH OF THE GOLF SWING

Ball aerodynamics
The dimples pull air along in the direction of the ball rotation, resulting in higher air speed (lower pressure) on top and lower air speed (higher pressure) at the bottom of the ball. The difference in air pressures give a lift force on the ball.

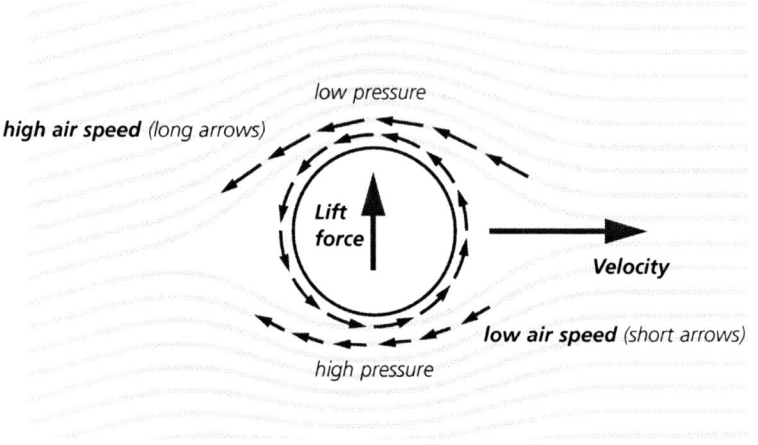

Did you know that?

Balls struck (by a good player) with a driver, a 3-iron, and a 9-iron reach almost identical heights? It is an optical illusion that the longer clubs produce a much lower trajectory, because the apex is farther away from the golfer.

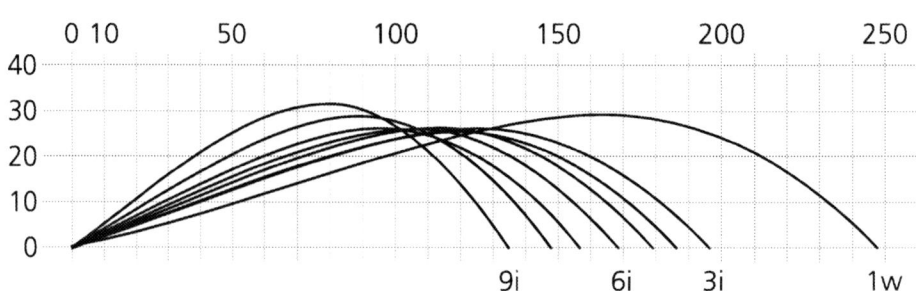

Height (in yards) vs carry (in yards) for various clubs.
Source: www.probablegolfinstruction.com

Curving shots

Most golf shots curve to one side – primarily because an absolutely straight shot is difficult to hit – so, there is no margin for error. Most of the time the clubface is slightly closed or open (seen from above) at impact, imparting sidespin as well as backspin on the ball. As the ball cannot spin in two directions simultaneously, a tilted backspin axis is the result and the ball curves through the air, the effect being strongest near the end of the flight where the forward momentum has decreased. Even shots hit with a square clubface but with hands too low or too high (or from stances where the feet are below or above the ball) curve through the air in the direction perpendicular to the clubface.

Use curving shots to your advantage

Good players use the almost inevitable sidespin in golf to their advantage. They groom a standard swing with a set-up that favors a particular ball flight. The trick is then to avoid hitting a shot with the opposite curve of the expected ball flight. This way the golfer in effect doubles the landing area. When a golfer always hits a draw, he takes aim down the right hand side of the fairway. A perfect, almost straight shot, ends up in the right side of the fairway. But even a big draw and a hook finds the fairway, one in the centre the other in the left side. Only a quick hook or anything right of target misses the fairway. This principle applies to every shot, pick a spot and move the ball toward the target. If the golfer is really gifted he can move the ball both left and right at will. This helps him get at difficult pin placements and hit drives around trees and other obstacles, but he may lack the consistency of the golfer who sticks to the same ball flight on every shot.

Air **resistance**

The flying ball is subjected to air resistance that decreases with low air density and increases with high air density. So, environments that are dry, dense, and cold are conductive to shorter shots, whereas the golfer enjoys longer shots in thin air and warm, damp conditions. These effects are quite noticable and certainly must be taken into consideration by better players. One hands-on figure states, that shots travel approximately 10 percent further in mountainous regions as compared to sea level.

Wind

The presence of wind has an even larger influence on the ball flight than atmospheric conditions. A wind assisted shot has a flatter trajectory with longer carry and lands "hotter" than normal, i.e. at a smaller angle. A head wind robs a shot of distance by increasing drag and promoting a ballooning trajectory. It doesn't take much wind to transform a 7-iron-shot into a 5-iron shot playing downwind, or into a 9-iron shot playing into the wind.

The wind speed rises with increasing height above ground, so when playing in strong winds, you must adjust the trajectory of your shots to get around the course without major calamities. In most situations, it is preferable to keep the shots low. A flat launch angle can be achieved consistently by placing the ball back in the stance and hitting it with the hands well in front of the ball at impact. It is not beneficial to hit the ball hard as this increases the backspin and, thus, lift and height which renders the ball to the mercy of the wind. Take at least two clubs more than you normally would, and swing shorter and slower. Only when playing downwind should you use your normal trajectory and you may find it beneficial to use 3-wood off the tee rather than driver in order to maximise the carry.

Control is alpha and omega when playing in strong winds. A following wind tends to blow the ball down and forward making it almost impossible to stop on the green, whereas side winds and head winds tend to blow the ball away from target and travel at too great a height, coming up short. You can either counteract side winds by aiming into the wind and allowing it to carry the ball back to target or you can spin the ball into the wind: playing a draw into a left-to-right wind and a fade into a right-to-left wind. The one thing to be avoided at all costs is hitting shots that spin in the same direction as the wind blows. A classic is the slice in a strong left-to-right wind. That ball is not likely to be seen again.

How far do you hit the ball?

The quest for distance seems to plague all golfers. A little silly given the far greater importance of precision, but I guess it can't be avoided – it's a macho thing. Most golfers hit the ball quite a lot shorter than they think. They seem to apply wishful thinking when they select an iron for an approach shot, or maybe they have just never bothered to measure their yardages.

"I once reached the green from here with a seven iron. Ergo the 7-iron is the club for the shot."

But often that 7-iron was a shot of a lifetime, or there was a strong following wind, or the shot was a flyer, or the ball barely made the green with the flag being miles further on. Whatever the cause, most golfers are **always short** on their approaches. They don't know their true average distance in carry with any club. And, this is a capital error in golf. To be a successful golfer, you must be 100 percent honest to yourself in judging your abilities and the shot at hand. You need to be humble when evaluating your capabilities. No golfer who overrates his potential is ever consistently successful.

CHAPTER 5 | THE SCIENTIFIC TRUTH OF THE GOLF SWING

It's probably **shorter** than you think

According to my observations, very few male amateurs with double-digit handicaps hit any iron shot on the fly further than 170 yards, on average. The differences in distance between their 5-, 4-, and 3-iron shots are negligible. The longer iron shots may fly lower and tend to roll more, but they don't soar like short iron shots. This is because you need both a precise strike and quite a lot of clubhead speed to generate lift and carry with the long irons. Most golfers simply **do not possess the required clubhead speed**. They would be better off taking the long irons out of the bag, concentrating on fairway woods or utility clubs for distance and ease of use.

Don't despair if you hit your iron shots short as compared to the professionals – they have to make a living from the game, you don't. Any handicap golfer who is consistent with the short irons has a chance to score well without being able to hit them a long way. But consistency as well as good swings come from swinging easy, not when you try to play shots that are beyond your ability.

Play **smart**

Don't carry a driver that produces an occasional bomb of 250 yards or more, mixed with a lot of worm-killers, slices or hooks. Settle for a 3-wood or a driver with at least 10.5 degrees of loft. The straight hitting golfer that averages 200 yards off the tee is in far better shape than the majority of his opponents. And, even the low handicapper has to shop around a lot for a driver that gives him both length and accuracy.

Back to the professionals – the equipment evolution together with the tough competition on the professional circuits has produced a very long hitting bunch. In addition, club manufacturers have taken to a trend of using stronger lofts on modern clubs, so that a pitching wedge today has the loft of a 9-iron of yesterday. Nevertheless, the numbers are impressive. A player like Ernie Els of South Africa carries his driver 280 yards, which was considered to be a good distance after roll on a firm fairway for the professionals. And, he hits his 9-iron 154 yards. This is the distance a long hitting player hit his 7-iron a few decades ago.

The need for **wedges**

But all this long hitting has a peculiar effect on the game; the professionals often "run out" of clubs. Because of their long drives – averaging around 280 yards including roll – they most often are left with no more than a short iron shot into the green, even on long par-4 holes. And, because they hit their irons a long way, they have very few to choose among. This is why the lob wedge (the most lofted club in the bag) and the gap wedge (the club with a loft in-between a sand iron and a pitching wedge) have become so popular in recent years. Most players prefer to use a full swing with a lob or gap wedge, rather than a half or three quarter swing with a sand iron or pitching wedge.

	Adam Scott	Justin Leonard	Tiger Woods	Vijay Singh	Phil Michelson
Driver	285	270	285	275	300
3-wood	250	235	265	250	270
4-wood		225			255
2-iron	235	220	245		
3-iron	220	215	230	220	230
4-iron	210	205	220	210	220
5-iron	200	190	208	195	205
6-iron	190	180	190	180	190
7-iron	175	165	172	165	175
8-iron	160	150	158	150	160
9-iron	150	140	142	140	150
PW	135	125	128	130	135
SW	115	105	106	115	110
LW	95	90	92	95	90

Carry distances in yards for some well known top golfers *(Source: Golf Digest)*

CHAPTER 5 | THE SCIENTIFIC TRUTH OF THE GOLF SWING

It is interesting to reflect on the fact that, the lob wedge covers a range from 0-90 yards and all remaining irons – up to a dozen of them – cover a similar sized range, from 90-220 yards. I think that the professionals, who spend most of their time practicing short shorts are very clever.

The Golfing **Gorillas**

Talking about length, I must mention the golfing gorillas of the longdriving tours. When they are on top of their game, they carry the ball past the 350 yard mark! This makes driving the green of par-4s possible in every round, and they expect to have a shot at the green in two on every par-5. It must be seen to be believed. If you want to hit the ball farther, it is a very good idea to study the longdrivers. These people have maxed out their potential and, contrary to popular belief, many of them have very sound golf swings. The swing mechanics of a guy like Carl Wolter is text book stuff – he just has more of everything than any other golfer. You must go to extremes to reach swing speeds of 150 mph, just like Carl does.

	Tiger Woods	Carl Wolter
Driver 1	310	375
Driver 2	285	325
3-wood	265	
2-iron	245	
3-iron	230	260
4-iron	220	245
5-iron	208	235
6-iron	190	220
7-iron	172	210
8-iron	158	195
9-iron	142	180
PW	128	150
SW	106	120
LW	92	90

Carry distances in yards for Tiger Woods and Carl Wolter, a "longdrive" champion
(Source: Golf Digest)

> *Most of the time he plays with the timidity of a middle-aged spinster walking home through a town full of drunken sailors, always choosing the safe side of the street.*
>
> – Peter Dobereiner (on Jack Nicklaus)

Chapter 6

May the **force** be with you

Due to the complicated nature of the golf swing and most golfer's less than adequate understanding of fundamental physics, there exists a great amount of misconceptions and fallacies as to how the energy of a good golf swing is created and transferred to the club. But the keen and ambitious golfer must have a clear and correct understanding of these fundamentals to obtain an efficient, precise, and reliable swing. (And, it certainly would help reduce the number of false golf prophets.)

The first important issue that I want to emphasise, is that the backswing is the preparation for the downswing, as the talented British professional John Garner eloquently puts it. You move the club back only to get it into a position from where you can propel it toward the ball. The faster you move the club back, the more force you have to apply to stop it at the top of the backswing to reverse direction for the downswing. It is, in consequence, almost impossible to swing the club back too slowly and of little benefit to swing fast.

The **hammer** analogy

Think of the way you would use a hammer to knock a nail into wood. You would never take the hammer back faster in order to hit the nail with greater force, instead, you would use a longer backswing and maintain control over the hammer in order to strike the nail (and miss your fingers).

To hit precisely in golf, it is essential to "swing within yourself" – that is, not to exceed your own speed limit. All golfers are not created equal, but everyone has a personal speed limit that shouldn't be exceeded.

The **gravity** analogy

To give the reader a short course in the concepts of force and energy, let's consider the effect of gravity on an object – for instance, Newton's famous apple. Gravity is a force that stems from the fact that masses attract. We golfers, with the possible exception of Alan Shepard – play on the surface of the Earth, where gravity is dominated by its huge mass. Here, all objects are subjected to Earth's gravitational field and are attracted with constant acceleration.

The force of gravity is **constant** but the speed increases

When you drop the infamous apple from shoulder height, the speed builds as it accelerates from the initial position at rest. Even though the force of gravity – the motor for the movement – remains constant, the apple accelerates. And, the greater the distance the apple falls, the greater the speed will be when it strikes the ground.

Defining **energy**

Energy, in classical physics, is defined as force multiplied by distance. The energy applied to the apple from gravity solely depends on the height fallen, because the gravitational acceleration (and the force on the apple) is constant. So, a constant force provides an amount of energy to an object that only depends on the distance over which the force acts.

Nothing groundbreaking in all of this, but try to imagine the golf swing in similar terms. The golf club substitutes the apple and you are the motor for the movement. If you apply whatever muscular force you are capable of producing **at a constant rate** during the downswing, the club accelerates and obtains a high speed without any need for "an explosive application of power," "a retention of the hit," or any other deliberate effect. A simple continuous muscular effort does the job admirably. And, the longer you take the club back, the more energy you apply to it during the downswing and the faster it travels at impact – without you hitting the ball harder.

You may have observed that, young people with limited muscular mass but great flexibility, often have long, "easy" swings and are able to hit the ball very far in relation to their strength. Conversely, players that are not able to take the club back very far, either because of a lack of flexibility or a lot of tension, need to be stronger (or hit harder) in order to generate clubhead speed. This is why golfers with muscular, heavily builds appear to hit rather than swing the club; they often turn very little, but they make up for the limited backswing by accelerating the club faster in the downswing. As the swing path is short and the acceleration large, the swing takes very little time to complete and is perceived as being a hit rather than a swing. But, it is fundamentally identical to a more gracious swing – dictated by the player's strength and physique.

So, this simple bio-mechanical principle works as a great equaliser – it levels the performance of golfers of different physiques. But, if a physically strong golfer is able to perform a big turn in his backswing, he has the potential to produce a huge amount of energy in the downswing and thus obtain very long shots. He needs strength, flexibility, lack of tension in the backswing and of course solid swing mechanics.

The **whiplash**-effect

Another important – and confusing – effect in the golf swing, that all good golf swings show to some extent the whiplash-effect, is described by physicists as *the conservation of angular momentum due to the golf swing being a two-lever system.*

What happens is that, kinetic energy (energy of motion) from the arms and shoulders is transferred to the club during the downswing, allowing the clubhead to obtain far greater velocity* than the handle. This effect only takes place when the clubhead is lagging the hands, and it can be hindered by the golfer by preventing the wrists from releasing freely. A highly strung golfer with a vice-like grip thus exhibits far less benefit from the whiplash-effect than a golfer with a loose, "wristy" swing. The important point to pick up is that the whiplash-effect happens automatically. It is simply the result of the club being swung in a circular arc with lag. When very good golfers state that they "whip the club through the ball at impact," they merely describe what

---

*) Strictly speaking, it is a greater **angular velocity**, because the clubhead is always travelling faster than the handle even with no wrist action, due to the circular motion of the swing.

takes place in their swings. The good golfer **allows** the club to release toward and through the ball, but he doesn't have to "hit" with his hands, *even though he may be inclined to think so.*

In fact, any deliberate wrist action toward the ball (in a full swing) will most likely ruin the shot because it destroys the whiplash-effect and the swing geometry. This is one of the cornerstones in understanding the golf swing.

Some people **will never learn**

Numerous are the professional golfers who have stated that the hands provide the power in the swing. But, it's simply not correct. They are all wrong – fooled by the whiplash-effect. Many intelligent arguments support the truth and ought to silence doubters – but that doesn't seem to happen. I guess the reason is that, you need to have faith in science and a scientific worldview to accept an explanation that, on the surface, seems to be counterintuitive.

I won't go into a lot of details here, as this whole study is squarely founded on the fact that the hands and arms play a passive role in a good golf swing, but I'll mention a few obvious facts:

a) Only the large muscles of the torso and legs can generate the energy required to power the swing.
b) If the arms alone supplied the energy, the golfer could hit further if he used his whole body.
c) All "hands and arms players" involve their bodies when they hit the ball. Why would they do that unless the body generates power?
d) The whiplash-effect (conserved angular momentum) is a real effect that you can't pretend doesn't exist. It is responsible for most of the observed "hand action" in "hands and arms players".

CHAPTER 6 | THE SCIENTIFIC TRUTH OF THE GOLF SWING

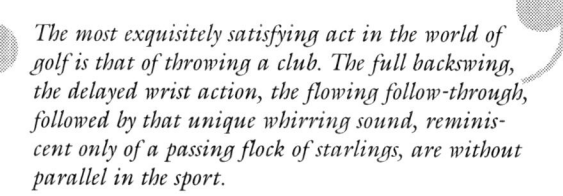

> *The most exquisitely satisfying act in the world of golf is that of throwing a club. The full backswing, the delayed wrist action, the flowing follow-through, followed by that unique whirring sound, reminiscent only of a passing flock of starlings, are without parallel in the sport.*
>
> – Henry Longhurst

Chapter 7

Notations & definitions

To be able to discuss technicalities in the golf swing, it is essential to have an identical understanding of the involved terms. My work is based on scientifically approved notations – so, when I use terms like "power" and "force," I refer to the scientific meaning – not some homemade reference to muscular or mental effort. But golf science suffers to a very large degree from a lack of unambiguous notations. In this chapter, I will define basic terms and principles.

Please note that the following notation is NOT the common way of describing open and closed stances. For some inexplicable reason, this term is defined illogically and incorrectly in most (if not all) golfing literature, resulting in fuzziness and confusion. With the correct notation, a closed clubface, stance, or shoulder line is always associated with balls going left and vice-versa for open clubface, stance, etc., and balls going right.

CHAPTER 7 | THE SCIENTIFIC TRUTH OF THE GOLF SWING

A **square** stance

A straight line running from the ball to the intended target is called the target line. A player that sets himself up with his shoulders, hips, and feet parallel to the target line is said to be aiming down the target line. This is also referred to as a square stance.

The square stance
The lines through the ball, the toes, and the shoulders are parallel and point to the target. The club shaft and clubface are perpendicular to the target line.

The clubhead is swung in a curve, the swing path, that is part of an inclined circle.

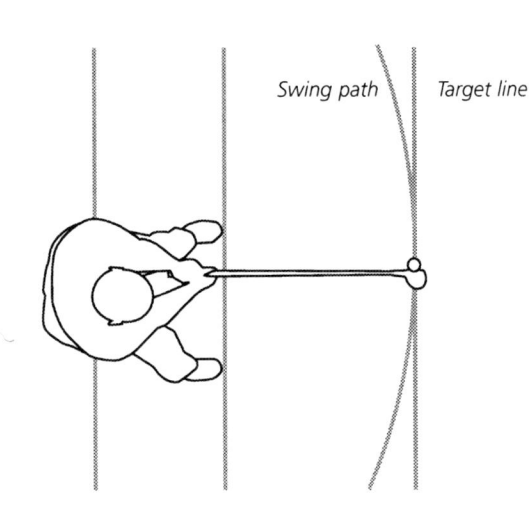

Swing path   Target line

NOTATIONS & DEFINITIONS | CHAPTER 7

Closed and opened stances

A player that sets himself up with his shoulders, hips, and feet pointing left of the target has therefore **closed his stance in relation to the target**. And, analogously, a player that sets himself up with his shoulders, hips, and feet pointing right of the target has opened his stance in relation to the target.

The open stance
The lines through the toes and the shoulders point right of the target. The club shaft and clubface are set perpendicular to the target line, but closed in relation the swing path and to the body orientation. This produces a shot that starts right of target and curves back toward the left – a draw.
As the ball is played further forward than a straight shot, the swing path becomes a bit longer and there is a tendency to hit the ball with the clubhead travelling parallel to the ground. This set-up is perfect for driving.

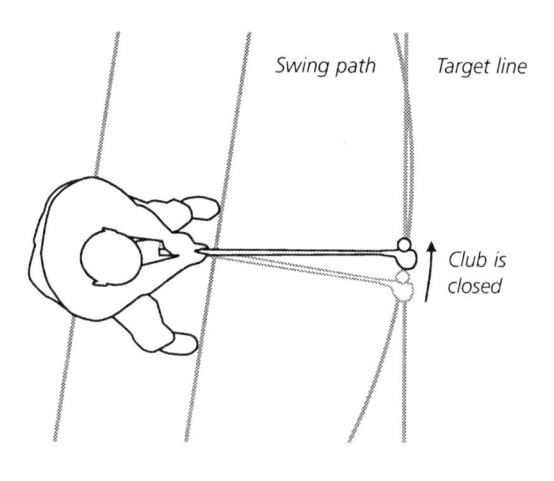

The closed stance
The lines through the toes and the shoulders point left of the target. The club shaft and clubface are set perpendicular to the target line, but open in relation the swing path and to the body orientation. This produces a shot that starts left of target and curves back toward the right – a fade.
As the ball is played further back than a straight shot, the swing path becomes a bit shorter and there is a tendency to hit the ball more in the downswing. This set-up is perfect for iron shots.

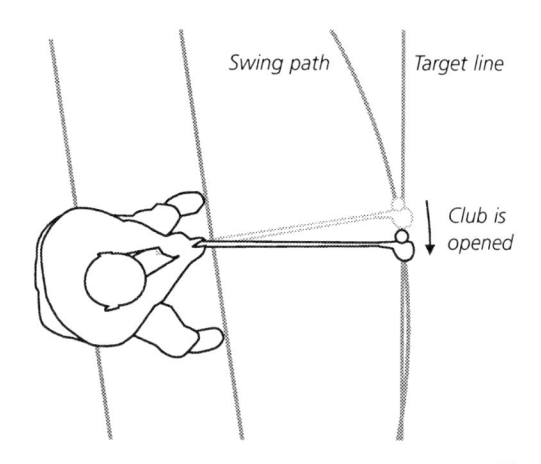

CHAPTER 7 | THE SCIENTIFIC TRUTH OF THE GOLF SWING

Clubface **orientation**

When the leading edge of the clubface is perpendicular to the target line, it is said to be in a square position. If it points left of target, it is said to be closed relative to the target line; if it points right of target, it is said to be open relative to the target line. But, we can also refer to the clubface orientation relative to the swing path – that is, relative to the direction of the clubhead's motion (the velocity vector). This makes a lot of sense, because it shows us whether the club is imparting sidespin on the ball. If the clubface is closed relative to the swing path (seen from above), the ball spins toward the left (in the direction that the clubface points), and if the clubface is open relative to the swing path (seen from above), the ball spins toward the right. A spin toward the left is called a draw (moderate) or a hook (pronounced), whereas spin toward the right is called a fade (moderate) or a slice (pronounced) – for a right handed player.

So, the player who sets up square to target with a square clubface and swings the clubhead toward the target at impact – in theory – hits a dead straight shot without any curvature (seen from above). If he aims left of target (uses a closed stance) and hits the same shot, it lands left of target. If he opens the clubface relative to the swing path, so that it is square to target, the shot starts out along the line of his stance but curves toward the right (fade), so that it lands in the vicinity of the target. Conversely, an open stance (aiming right of target) with the clubface oriented toward the target (closed clubface in relation to swing path) results in a draw that works its way back toward the target.

Any rotary movement of the club into the backswing evokes an opening of the clubface in relation to the target line, but not necessarily in relation to the swing path. It is theoretically possible to swing the club so that the clubface always stays square to the swing path, called a "square-to-square" swing. An example is a short "put" performed primarily with the shoulders, without any wrist action whatsoever. But, for a number of reasons, it is impossible to hit a full shot with a square-to-square swing.

The swing plane

There are several conflicting opinions regarding what a swing plane is and especially what it should be. I'll simply define the swing plane as the (geometric) plane that is described by the club shaft during the swing. My reason for this is, that at impact, the objective is to return the club to the address position. And, for the ball to be hit straight toward target, the clubhead has to travel on a curve that, at impact, has a tangent pointing to target (and possibly slightly downward). This plane has the inclination of the

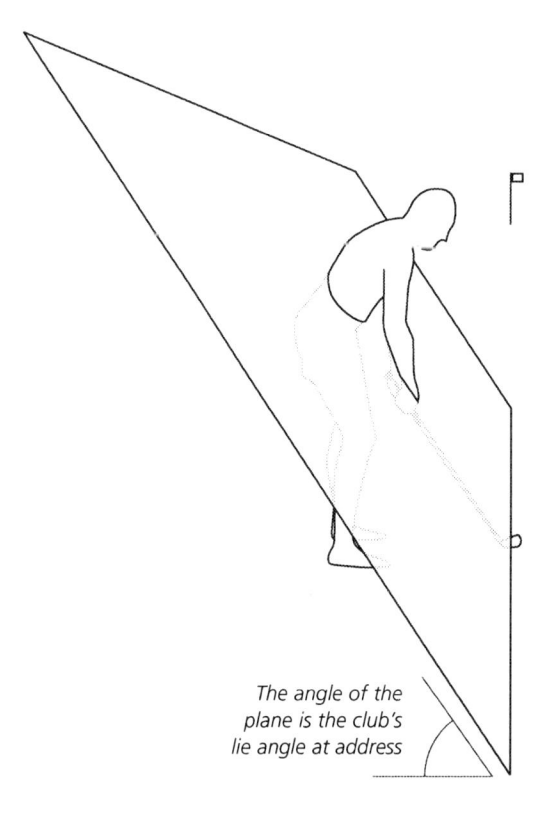

The swing plane at address is determined by the golf club's shaft and the target line (when hitting a straight shot). It can be envisioned as a big pane of glass bisecting the golfer (courtesy of Ben Hogan).

The angle of the plane is the club's lie angle at address

club's lie angle and is parallel to the target line. Like Ben Hogan suggested in his book "The Modern Fundamentals of Golf," you can envision it as being a great pane of glass that bisects the player.

So, just before impact, the club has to move in this plane, and, therefore, both hands and clubhead lie in the plane, being at opposite ends of the shaft. But, in the backswing, the start of the downswing and the follow-through, the club can swing in any arbitrary plane. I'll present a case for the advantages of always trying to swing in one single plane in the end of Chapter 9, but the main importance of the swing plane concept is that it provides us with a frame of reference for describing how a player swings a club. When he deviates from the impact/address swing plane, we can easily describe what he has done with reference to the swing plane, and what effects this has on the shot.

Did you know...

Ben Hogan had an extremely long and markedly upright swing when he was a struggling young professional in the 1930s (quite similar to present day's John Daly) – he only found success after he changed to a much flatter swing plane (shaft plane). Not surprising that it is he who is credited with inventing the "swing plane" concept – it is perfect for illustrating how he changed his own swing. But Hogan's new "flat" swing was still very long with a lot of wrist rotation and cupping. It is a common misconception that flat swings are shorter than steep swings – they merely exhibit less lifting of the arms in the backswing and, therefore, appear to be short when viewed face-on.

> *Maybe Fuzzy Zoeller plays golf the way everybody should. Hit it, go find it, hit it again. Grin, have a smoke, take a sip, make a joke and every so often win a major championship.*
>
> – Dan Jenkins

Chapter 8

Practical guide – **Preparations**

Traditional golf books and instructional articles invariably fail to give a complete picture of what the golf swing is all about. They talk about stance, posture, grip, takeaway, top-of-backswing, impact, and follow-through as if these elements are not related. In reality they are woven together: You can't change any element without it having an effect on others.

Thus, the search for a good swing becomes a matter of trial and error in compiling dozens of variables – each with many possible actions. And, because the unhappy player cannot possibly focus on more than one or two movements during a swing, it is all but impossible to piece together a solid repeatable action by trial and error.

CHAPTER 8 | THE SCIENTIFIC TRUTH OF THE GOLF SWING

Always ask **WHY?**

A far better way of progressing is to apply a holistic view of the golf swing. Don't accept advice from anyone prepared to offer it without first asking WHY?

Why do I need to
    ...grip the club loose?
    ...use a weak grip or a strong gri?
    ...shift my weight from one foot to another?
    ...swing from inside to outside or inside to inside?
Or whatever the advice may be.

Every piece of the swing must fit precisely together and the player must know how. This study shows that even very, very good professional players (and swing coaches) often don't have a clue about how they swing the club. They tend to rationalize the swing using terms and beliefs that, upon closer examination, show to be poorly defined and therefore inapplicable or just plain wrong.

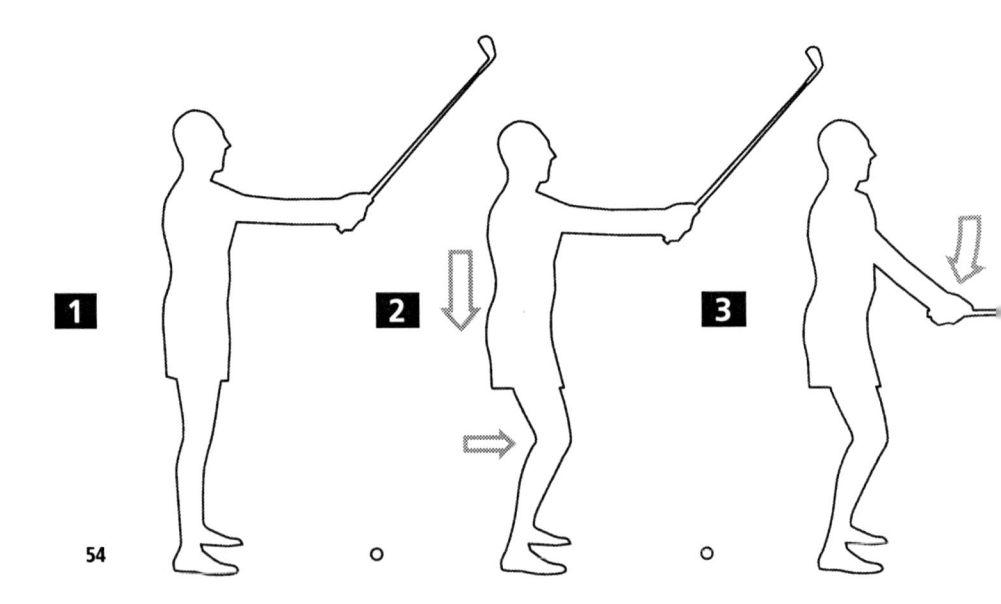

PRACTICAL GUIDE – PREPARATIONS | CHAPTER 8

The instructions in this study do not describe one perfect golf swing, nor do they claim that there exists one perfect fit-all-swing.

But they describe the fundamentals that the best golfers in the world have used in their swings ever since the technology of club and ball manufacturing reached a level comparable to modern standards. This study also analyzes which degrees of freedom a golfer has in building his individual swing, how these individual traits show themselves, and what their effects are for the golfer.

The basics of a good swing are simple to learn, provided that a simple approach is used. For the purpose of teaching and understanding, the golf swing can be broken down into two required elements, *the body rotation* and *the arm movement*. But, neither element exists without the other in a good swing. The body rotation is a very simple motion with few possible (or desired) variations. The arm movement is what gives character to a golfers swing – there is a great number of possible – but not required – variations.

But, before we can discuss the swing itself, we need to address the ball correctly – we need a good set-up.

David Leadbetter's routine for getting into a proper address position
(Refer to text for details)

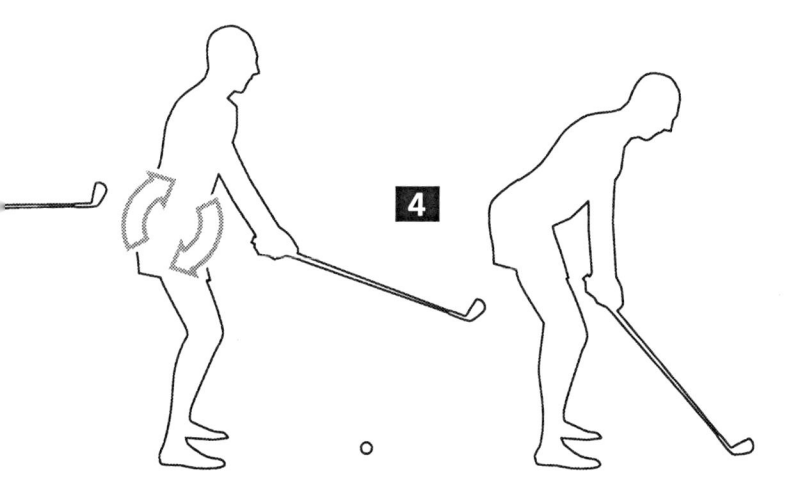

55

CHAPTER 8 | THE SCIENTIFIC TRUTH OF THE GOLF SWING

Setting up in an **alert posture**

The most important characteristic of the address position is that the body should be poised in an alert position with muscles ready to spring into action. A good mental image is a tennis player ready to receive a serve. Somewhat crouched, in balance, knees bent, focused, alert, never completely without motion. The main issue here is that the lower body should be on the ready.

The very successful golf instructor David Leadbetter can be credited with a good routine to get into a proper address position:

1 Stand upright, grip the club and hold your arms and the club horizontally in front of you.
2 Flex the knees so your legs are comfortably "springy."
3 Let your arms drop until they are stopped by your chest.
4 Bend from the waist (by rotating your pelvis) until the club hits the ground. You should feel balanced and capable of resisting attempts that might push you off balance.

Such a recipe is, of course, not foolproof – it requires personal adaptation and a lot of practice to repeat without deviations. But, it represents a very good starting point. The arms should feel pretty immobile in a good set-up and this is entirely correct. We want to minimize all unnecessary arm movement.

In a poor set-up, the arms are typically loose and have a lot of room to move, whereas the body tends to be crouched, cramped, and locked – simply because the handicap golfer focuses on using his arms rather than the entire body.

The **left** hand **grip**

The body is the driving force in the swing, so the role of the hands becomes secondary and the grip doesn't have the importance that many instructors preach. Obviously, a good player's grip is important to him because it works with his particular swing and produces the results he expects. But, he could equally well have learned a different grip which would also produce good results, but with a different set-up, different ball trajectory, etc. Therefore, one particular grip cannot be recommended and this fact is evident looking at the best players in the world. They use a wide variety of individual grips.

But, we can pinpoint some of the features that characterizes a good grip.

One important point to note is that, an efficient golf swing has lag – the shaft lags the arms in the downswing. So, a good grip allows the lag by allowing the wrists to cock, to use an old fashioned term. This wristcock is partly a clockwise rotation of the underarms and partly a bending of one or both wrists. By experimentation, you'll probably find that the required freedom of the wrists is best achieved by gripping the club in the fingers rather than the palms, letting the club run more across than diagonally through the left hand.

You'll also need a "solid" left hand grip that gives you control over the club even when gripping lightly. The reason is that the forces acting on the club during the swing are large, so you automatically grab the club tighter in the downswing and thereby risk unwanted club manipulations by the hands. The grip should allow the wrists to be flexible and passive, even when swinging hard at the ball. Test this by gripping the club as tightly as you can and observe what happens to the clubface. A good grip allows you to strangle the club without the clubface opening or closing.

The **right** hand **grip**

The position of the right hand should be almost exclusively dictated by the left hand grip, as the right hand has more contact with the left hand than with the club. It is beneficial to keep both hands close together by using an overlapping or interlocking grip, and the grip should be very light to the extent that the right hand can leave the grip altogether during impact – thrown off by the rapid, but passive, release through impact.

The set-up **geometry**

The set-up position depends on which club is used and the desired trajectory of the shot. Seen from the front, or "face-on," the ball should be placed somewhere between the chin and the left shoulder for a standard shot. It is a very bad idea to determine the ball position in relation to the feet, because the width of the stance then has to be taken into the equation.

Consider two golfers, one using a very narrow stance and the other a very wide stance, and tell them to play the ball inside the left heel. One would then have the ball positioned in the centre of his stance, while the other would play it opposite his shoulder – two vastly different ball positions. It is much more precise to indicate the ball position in relation to the head and shoulders.

If the ball is played far forward (toward target), it becomes difficult to hit it with the hands leading the clubhead. You will have difficulty taking turfs and your shots will have a high trajectory.

If the ball is played back in the stance, it is natural to hit it with the hands well in front of the ball, de-lofting the club and producing low shots. You will also have a tendency to take big turfs and have trouble getting your long shots airborne.

The spine, when viewed face-on, should be vertical or leaning away – never leaning toward the target. Leaning the spine away from target is totally analogous to hitting the ball more from inside – thus, it's worth a try if you have problems coming over the top. The width of the stance should be at least shoulder width for any full shot and can possibly be very wide for the longer clubs. The golfer should think more about the angles of the legs with vertical rather than actual measures. Thus, a golfer with long legs should stand wider than one with shorter legs. I see no reason at all that a long legged golfer should limit his stance to shoulder width just to comply with some arbitrary "rule," because a narrow stance severely limits the maximum power his legs can produce by restricting his leverage.

The spine, when viewed down the line, should be kept as straight as comfortably possible, because this facilitates a simple turn without unnecessary movements.

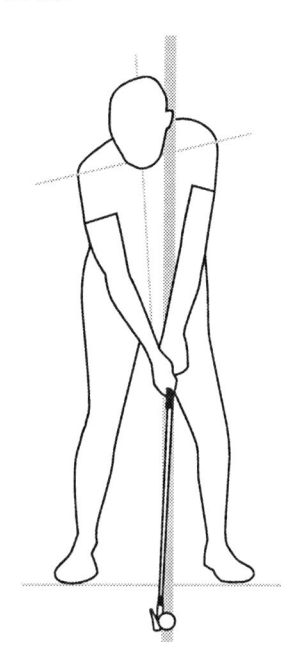

The ball position
The ball position should be evaluated relative to the head (and spine), NOT relative to the feet.

The golfer at the top plays the ball close to the center of his stance, whereas the golfer below plays the ball upposite his left heel. But, in reality, they both play the ball in the identical position relative to the head and spine, which is the axis that the swing revolves around.

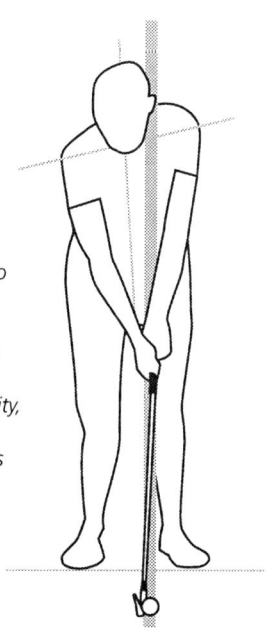

CHAPTER 8 | THE SCIENTIFIC TRUTH OF THE GOLF SWING

A note about the distance from the ball: Through experimentation, notice that you can shift your center of gravity along a line pointing to the ball.

This means that your spine and club shaft angles remain constant, and that only the angles of your ankles, knees, and hips change. You'll see that you are able to "slide" the clubface into position behind the ball by leaning forward and backward. When you slide forward, toward the ball, your center of gravity moves along and your weight distribution shifts toward your toes. Conversely, you can bring your weight toward your heels by "sliding" away from the ball. It is very hard, if not impossible, to give concrete advice as to how far away from the ball a player should stand. Some great players stand very close to the ball and others very far away. The best stance is a compromise between your physical capabilities and your swing dynamics, and can only be found through experimentation an the range.

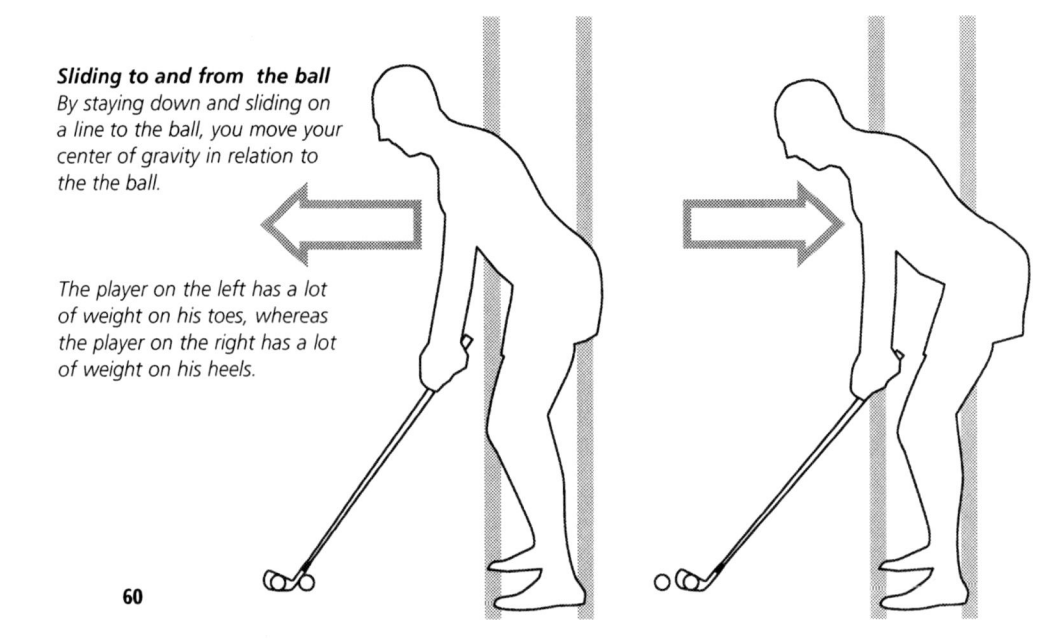

Sliding to and from the ball
By staying down and sliding on a line to the ball, you move your center of gravity in relation to the the ball.

The player on the left has a lot of weight on his toes, whereas the player on the right has a lot of weight on his heels.

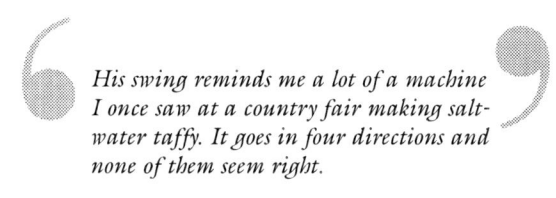

> *His swing reminds me a lot of a machine I once saw at a country fair making salt-water taffy. It goes in four directions and none of them seem right.*
>
> – Buck Adams (on Miller Barber)

Chapter 9

Practical guide
– The swing

There are two primary motions in a golf swing, *the body rotation* and *the arm movement.*

The body rotation provides most of the power and control, while the arm movement makes sure that the club is in a proper position to be swung at the ball.

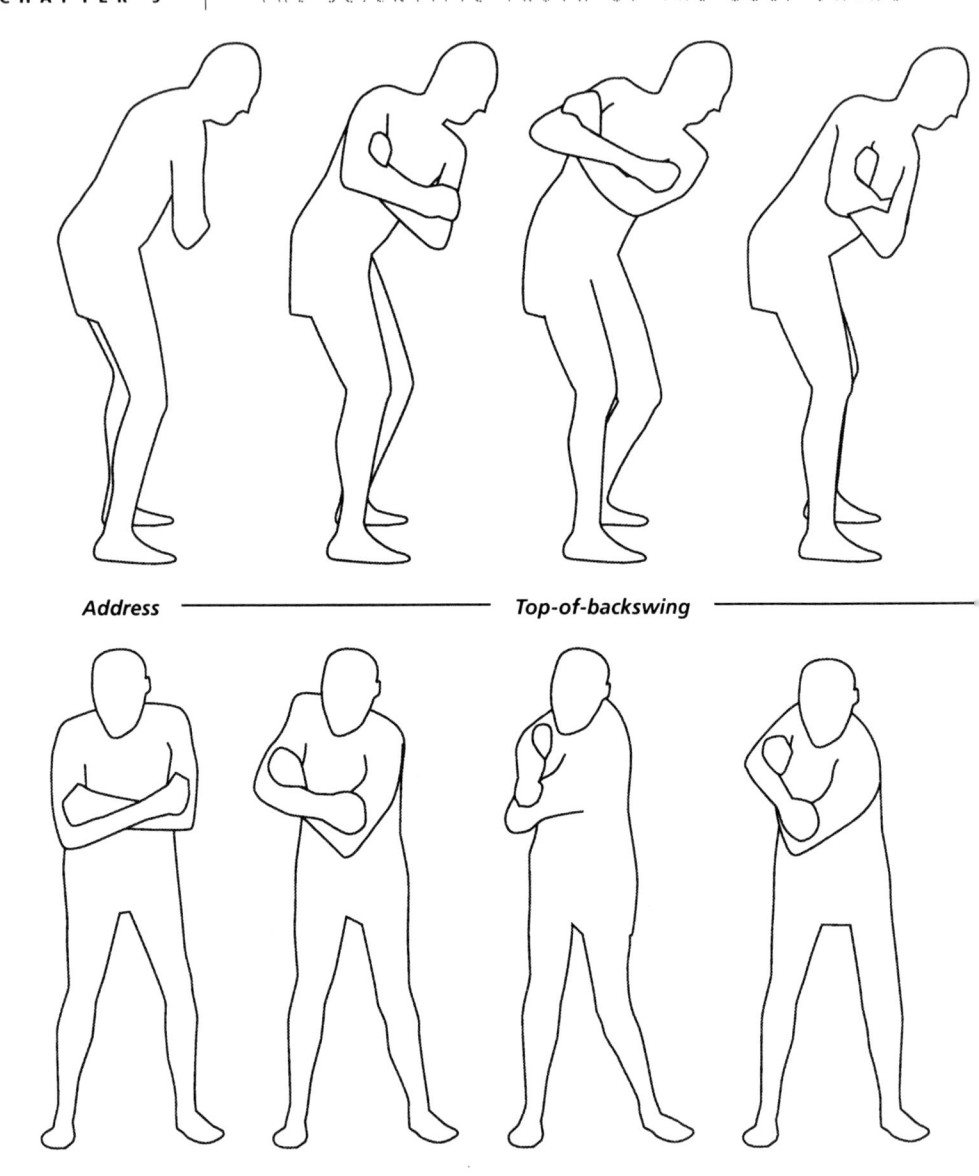

CHAPTER 9 | THE SCIENTIFIC TRUTH OF THE GOLF SWING

Address ——————————— **Top-of-backswing** ———————

The body **rotation**

The body movement can be described as "a turning of the shoulders by the legs." The hips also turn to some extent – determined by the players build, his suppleness and tension, the length of his limbs, and various other parameters. The main question is not how much the hips turn, but how the legs are initiating and controlling the turn. The

PRACTICAL GUIDE – THE SWING | CHAPTER 9

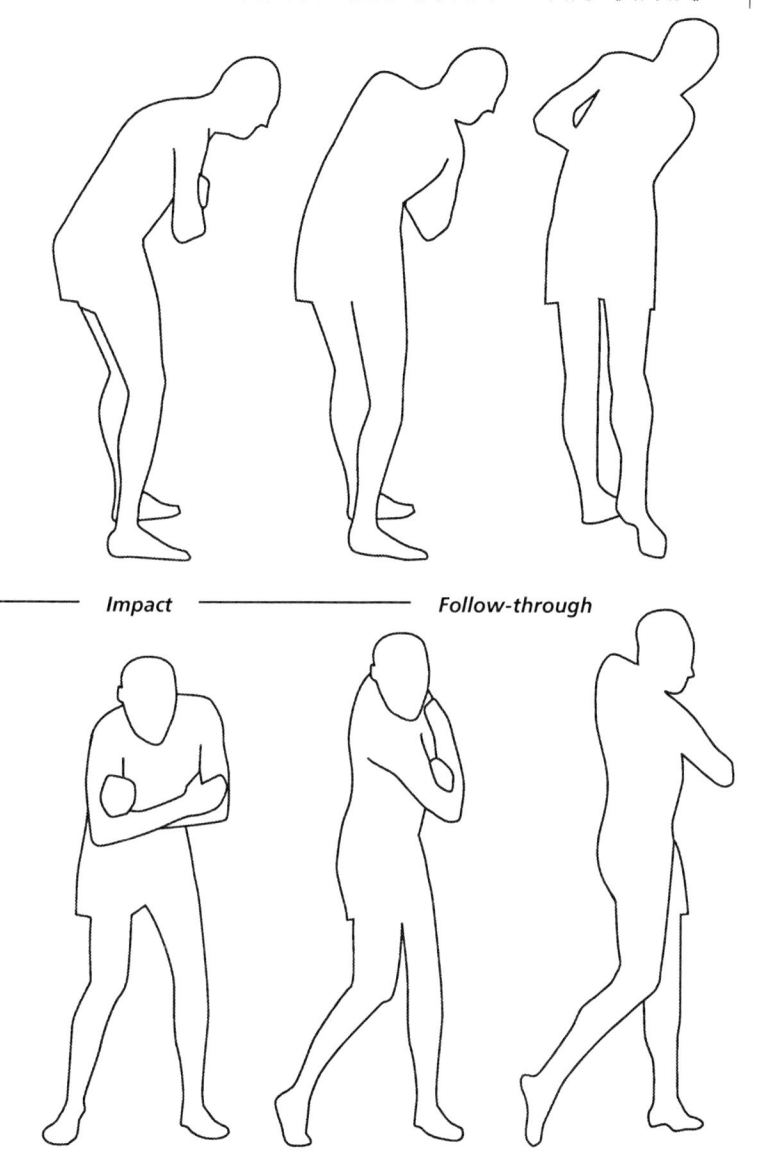

Impact —————————— Follow-through

objective for the shoulders is to turn as far as comfortably possible; most golfers of average build should have no problems turning 90 degrees – that is "turning their back to the target" – provided that they keep tension out of the turn. **Tension does not produce power,** because energy can't be stored in muscles and tendons. The sole objective for a big turn in the backswing is to create room for the legs to work during the downswing – before the ball is hit.

The left **heel**

Through the years, there has been a lot of debate regarding whether the left heel should stay on the ground or should leave the ground. My conclusion is: Who cares? Try it out and stick with what works for you. If you use a very wide stance, it is almost impossible not to lift the heel, but for narrower stances you have a choice. One intelligent argument is for lifting the left heel on every shot with a full swing, which forces the player to initiate the downswing by planting the left heel, thus, preventing an active upper body at the start of the downswing. This is what the legendary Bobby Jones always did. It is very evident that his pronounced heel lift not was a result of straining his backswing, but simply a visible swing key ingrained in his swing.

The **axis** of rotation

The axis of rotation should be thought of as the spine or an axis parallel to the spine located behind the golfer. Please observe that this is merely a mental image; in reality, the upper body moves freely along with the lower body and the true centerline of the rotation moves along with it. Don't ever try to swing like a machine with strictly defined movements around a fixed axis – you are not a machine, so don't behave like one. Video footage and multi-exposure photos of good players show that the hands describe a circular motion – in some cases a perfect circle – but the center of the rotation is not, and should not be, the spine or the left shoulder or any other body part.

This main movement of the golf swing should resemble the athletic discipline of hammer throwing, where the athlete and the hammer are always in dynamic balance during the speed-build-up phase preceding the launch. The thrower pulls the hammer and the hammer pulls the thrower, each with (almost) identical forces. Consequently, the center of rotation is an axis placed somewhere between the thrower and the hammer – but nearer the thrower because he is heavier than the hammer. For the golfer this can be described in the sentence, *you are not swinging the club, you are swinging together with the club!*

The body rotation can and should be practised without the arm movement. And, the golfer should train himself to identify the body rotation when studying golf swings. No matter how fast the hands and the club are moving, behind them the true power source controls the swing at a much more leisurely pace.

Propeller aircraft **analogy**

A propeller aircraft is an interesting analogy to the golf swing. The only visible moving part – apart from the plane itself – is the propeller, which rotates rapidly and makes a lot of noise due to the air flow around it. The propeller does a lot of work (in the physicist's sense of the word) and has a tremendous amount of rotational energy (if it were to fall off, it would cause some serious damage). But, the propeller does not contribute any energy at all to the motion – it doesn't contain an energy source. All energy comes from the engine and is transmitted via the drive shaft through the propeller to the air. This is exactly what takes place in the golf swing: The majority of energy is generated by the large muscles of the body – chiefly by a rotating movement in relation to the ground – and is transmitted to the golf club through the arms. To the bystander, it appears that the arms have to work hard, because they move much faster than the body. But in reality, they do not need to generate energy, they only have to transmit the body's energy, just like the propeller transmits the engine's energy. So, the true function of the arms is to be in a position to transmit energy to the club, and the required arm tension is a function of the quality of the swing geometry.

CHAPTER 9 | THE SCIENTIFIC TRUTH OF THE GOLF SWING

In a perfect, on-plane golf swing (think for instance of Michelle Wie), you can have almost limb arms; but, if the swing geometry is poor, you need to "work" the club a lot with your hands and arms.

Proof of the true role of the arms can be found when studying action photos of longhitters at the moment of impact: The right arm is still bent – it almost retains the top-of-backswing position. So, the arms can't have contributed energy to the club because their relative position is unchanged – they have not released. But, through the body movement, they have been brought from the top of the backswing position to the impact position. The actual release, where both arms are extended and the clubface rolls over, takes place **after impact**, when the ball is well on its way.

This wonderful picture of Hank Kuehne from the cover of Golf Digest epitomises the essence of a good golf swing:
Hank, who is a very long hitter, has rotated his body so that his hips almost face the target at impact. His shoulders lag the hips a lot and his right arm has not straightned fully at impact. As the torso almost retains the full coil from the top of the backswing and the arms haven't released, it is evident that the legs have worked tremendously during the downswing, rotating the hips approximately 135 degrees into the shot. Thus, the legs are the major power source in Hank's swing.

The fact that the arms are passive does not mean that their role is of minor importance. On the contrary, their most distinguished role is to make sure that the club is in a good position at the top of the backswing, from where it can be propelled powerfully toward the ball and hit it squarely in perfect geometry. When the club is properly placed just before impact (in the late hit position), the whiplash-effect contributes to clubhead speed, by transferring further energy to the club.

Head-spinning thoughts

Even though the thought of swinging around your spine is a great mental image, it is not exactly what takes place in reality. When the body turns in relation to the ground (and ball), the head tends to follow the movement of the body. This means that keeping the head still during the swing necessitates an active turning of the head, counter-clockwise during the backswing and clockwise during the forward swing. Thus, a head kept passively still would swivel during the swing, and a player who is accredited with holding his head still is actually turning his head back and forth very precisely during the swing to counter the movement of the body. Observe that many players, most notably Anika Sörenstam and David Duval, allow their head to turn with the body into the ball, so that they do not look directly at the ball when striking it. I can thoughly recommend that you pre-turn your head in the direction of the backswing (clockwise) to make room for the shoulder turn. This move, used and recommended by Jack Nicklaus and Sam Snead, among others, can really make the difference between a cramped, uncomfortable position at the top and a smooth, comfortable backswing.

The downswing

After reaching the top of the backswing at maximum shoulder turn, the downswing commences. Here, it is essential that the legs initiate the movement. There has to be some kind of leg action, often described with that dreadful term "weight shift," but it's far better to mainly concentrate on having the legs rotate the body into the shot, not starting the powerful leg drive before the legs are in a proper position. Think of the participants in a game of tug of war. If they don't brace themselves in an alert position before the start, they will be swept off their feet at once. They cannot apply their power to the rope without a proper footing – and exactly the same is true in the downswing. As many instructors and golf writers have pointed out, this is the position that makes or breaks swings. Some instructors talk about "gripping the ground with your feet," and great swingers like Nick Faldo and Sam Snead have been seen barefooted on the range, because this excersise really makes you aware of what your feet are doing.

In the downswing, you should focus on keeping up the rotation until your body faces the target to avoid quitting on the shot. You might argue that once the ball has been hit, it is of little consequence what you do. That's perfectly correct, but the issue here is that due to the very rapid progression of the swing, the golfer is only aware of having made contact with the ball when he is well into his finish, and then he must stop the turning anyway. In other words, if the golfer tries to stop his deliberate turn when he hits the ball, he gravely risks quitting on the shot.

Lastly, a comment about the pace of the body movement. It obviously sets the pace for the entire swing, but everything should take place at a comfortably slow pace for the player. The body must not loose control over the swing and it doesn't have to, because even a very leisure body swing can produce tremendous arm and club speed.

The arm **movement**

The correct, necessary role of the hands and arms in the swing is far more subdued and different than general knowledge and intuition suggests. If there is a secret in golf that eludes most players – even very good ones – it is the role of arms and hands. It can be described as follows:

PRACTICAL GUIDE – THE SWING | CHAPTER 9

Take your stance, keep the shoulders immobile, and your left arm reasonable straight. Now try bending the right elbow to a 90 degree angle. You will find that this can only be done comfortably by allowing the left arm a similar rotation of 90 degrees, the reason being that your grip limits

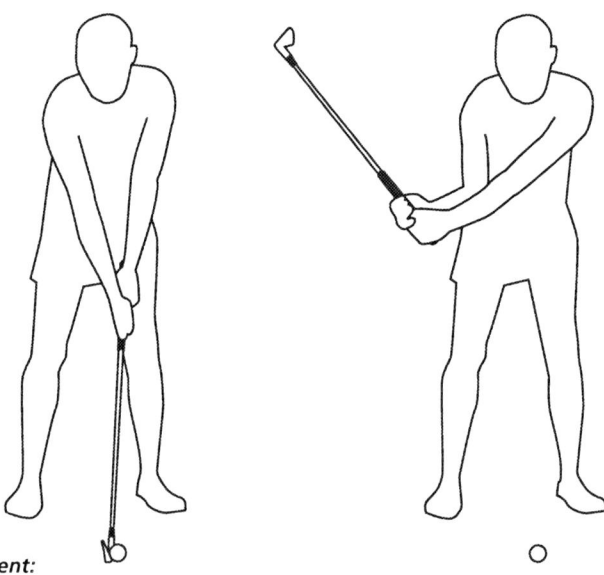

The arm movement:
This is the only required movement of the arms and hands during a good golf swing. Combine this action with a body turn for the full swing.

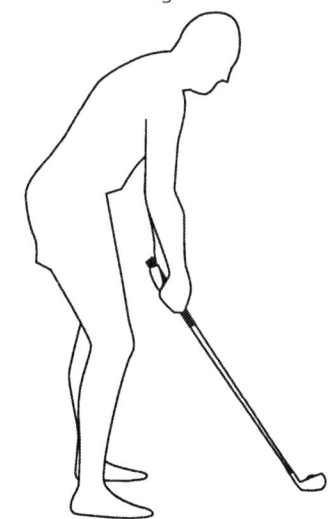

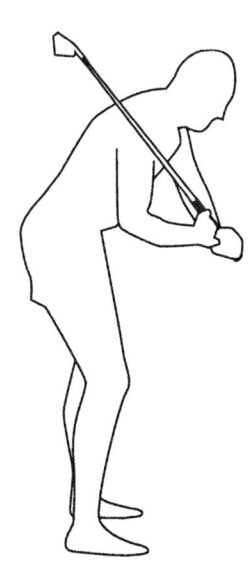

the freedom of your arms. This is perfectly acceptable, in fact preferable, as it prevents the club from taking up a poor position. Your right elbow ends up close to your side and the shaft of the club points in the direction of your backswing. This is the only *necessary* movement of the arms and hands.

Try superimposing the body move by turning your body into the backswing; you should find yourself in a perfect top of the backswing position. From here, you can turn your body into the downswing without further ado. You don't have to wait for the arms to "drop into the slot" or any other move, because the club is already ideally positioned on-plane to be swung at the ball.

The flower power era: **"Get high"**

This is not the case in the much steeper swing that was popular in the 1970s, no doubt because of Jack Nicklaus' immense success with a rather untraditional style. One of Jack's swing keys was to "reach for the sky" during the backswing – to lift his hands as high as possible away from the ball. This obviously produces both a very steep swing plane, a well as a top of the backswing position from where it is nearly impossible to avoid coming over the top during the forward swing. This Jack used to his advantage by securing a large fade on practically every shot in the bag, but it is definitely not a position to recommend to the average golfer who, more than anything, wants to hit his shots with a draw. Therefore, I recommend using a minimum of "arm lift" during the backswing.

You can experiment with using "high hands" in a similar way as above. Take your stance and make the minimal arm swing by rotating the left arm and folding the right elbow (illustrated on the previous page). From here, you can hardly move your hands any lower (that is, achieve a flatter position at the top) because your right elbow touches your stomach or hip. But, you can indeed lift your arms way up to the level of your head. When applying the body turn, you'll find yourself in a "classic" 1970s position – an ungainly "high hands" position from where you can only swing down very steeply at the ball. Slicers of the world unite and stay away from this position – the correct downswing motion by the body inevitably results in a slice or pull from this position.

The main **cause** of the **slice**

Thus, it is the backswing that sets up the slice, not the downswing, and the only way to prevent the slice is to introduce an extra parameter, a patch to the swing. This could be a blocking motion of the arms, preventing them from releasing freely (which would also introduce tension and probably rob the shot of distance), or it could be a strong move of the legs in the direction of the target (a race to keep the club from closing too early). The important lesson to grasp here is that "high hands" really don't provide more power to a swing, but favors a fade or slice and quite possibly a need for a correcting action. It worked admirably for Nicklaus, but it probably won't work for you!

By studying the "minimal arm action, no body swing position" more thoroughly, notice that there is one additional degree of freedom available in the backswing: The possibility of cocking the left wrist at an angle to the left forearm. If you only rotate the left wrist, the wrist is almost in line with the lower arm, "flat," but it can obtain an angle of 50 degrees or so, depending on the your flexibility. This wrist cock, "cupping" as it is sometimes referred to, is necessary if the golfer seeks the renowned ultra late hit position that Ben Hogan was famous for, and that Sergio Garcia from Spain also favors in his swing. Mind you, it doesn't have to lead to the very extreme late hit position, but it is a prerequisite. With this "extra" wrist cock, the club lags the hands even more than the result of the left arm rotation, thus delaying the hit and giving the body more time and room to power the club before impact. The club is, so to speak, "opened" even more relative to the body.

It is also interesting to note that a strong and/or firm right hand grip restricts the cocking of the left wrist greatly, maybe even forcing it into a position with the left wrist bowed outward. This is the real cause that a strong right hand grip can lead to a hook – it tends to firm up and shorten the backswing, producing a top-of-backswing position where the club is not lagging the hands very much. From such a position, a simple (rotating) downswing produces hooks and pulls because the club catches up with the hands – it has a shorter distance to travel than if it had been opened more.

The shoulders, arms, hands, and club **move as one unit** in the downswing

During the downswing, until a very short time before impact, the shoulders, arms, hands, and club are placed in an almost unchanged relative position – that is, they move as one unit rotating together with the body. To keep this relative position intact when the movement picks up speed, angular velocity to be precise, the arms and hands have to **prevent the club from releasing** by actively maintaining the coiled position. This again is directly in opposition to the preachings of the many golf instructors who state that the golfer should "throw the clubhead at the ball," "whip the club through with the right hand," have "speedy hands" and so on. The truth is, many good golfers make an active effort with their hands **against the centrifugal force** to ensure that the club doesn't release prematurely.

A proof of the correctness of this can be found in the paradox, that the most common fault among handicap golfers is to release the club too early in an attempt to produce clubhead speed. When presenting their problem to their golf professional, they are told – correctly – to delay the hit (or release) with the arms until later in the swing, but trying to do this without a corresponding body swing obviously robs them of most clubhead speed. The body absolutely has to work hard early in the downswing to produce great clubhead speed, and this is very evident when you watch good players swing. They do not beat around the bushes, but "drive" hard toward and through the ball from the top of the swing **with the body**.

The backswing path – and why it is of **minor importance**

As stated previously, the sole role of the backswing is to place the club in a position where it can be swung at the ball, mainly through the counter-clockwise rotation of the body. Thus, it is very important to be in a proper position at the top of the backswing, but HOW you get there is of minor importance. This is really the only part of the swing where the golfer can deviate from "the norm" without major ill effects.

To some extent, the backswing is determined through contemporary prevalence rather than strict necessity. It's a fashion statement! In the era of Bobby Jones, every good player seemed to drag the clubhead away from the ball as the last element to commence motion in the backswing. This requires a lot of "wristiness" and is impossible to do properly if you grip the club too tight. It could partially be a result of the use of hickory shafted clubs (with relative flexible shafts and low torsion rigidity), but many golfers kept doing this after the advent of steel shafted clubs.

CHAPTER 9 | THE SCIENTIFIC TRUTH OF THE GOLF SWING

In the 1970s and 1980s, the "one-piece takeaway" was being hailed as the seventh wonder in golf, and this was the trademark of many professionals of that era; no doubt because a one-piece takeaway helps in achieving a very steep top-of-backswing position.

In recent years, there has been a tendency to revert to a more rounded, flatter swing, where the left arm is allowed to break down producing a nice position at the top almost without tension. I think that this is both a natural and positive evolution that eliminates the unnatural and unnecessary elements of sliding the lower body toward the target and, not least the resulting, backbreaking "reverse-C" position. To the best of my knowledge, these features don't have any advantages over the so called modern (rounded) swing, which, incidentally, was well known and used by a lot of players in the 1950s and 1960s.

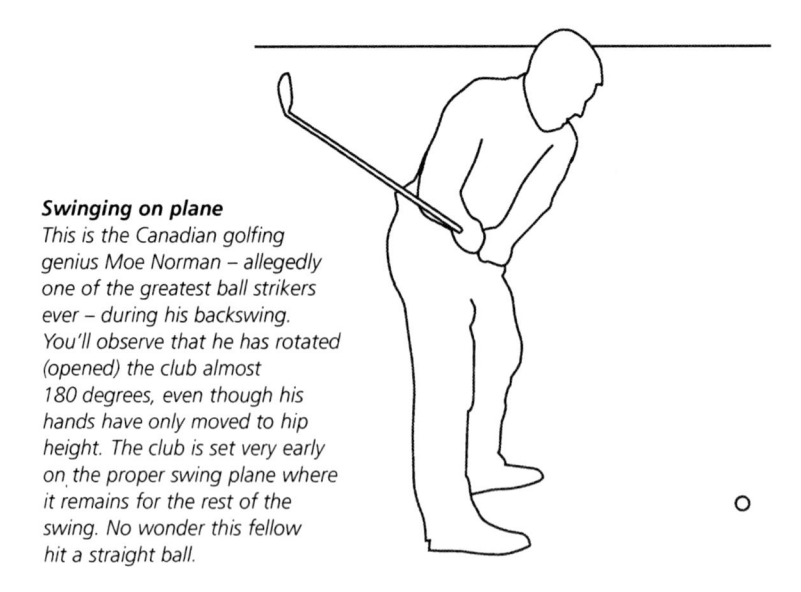

Swinging on plane
This is the Canadian golfing genius Moe Norman – allegedly one of the greatest ball strikers ever – during his backswing. You'll observe that he has rotated (opened) the club almost 180 degrees, even though his hands have only moved to hip height. The club is set very early on the proper swing plane where it remains for the rest of the swing. No wonder this fellow hit a straight ball.

The benefits of swinging **on plane**

To be totally honest, it is impossible to swing precisely in only one plane during a swing. But, taken with a grain of salt, it is possible to come very close. The best way of checking your swing plane is to use a video camera placed chest high directly behind the ball, and recording down the line. When you swing on plane, your club shaft points at the ball. When you're not on plane, your club shaft points anywhere else.

I have found that there are three major advantages to swinging on plane, or at least trying to swing on plane:

1. **Simplicity**

At impact, the club has to be on plane (when hitting a straight shot that starts toward target). Therefore, the club has to be brought onto the plane during the downswing, if it is not already on plane at the top of the backswing. This calls for a manipulation of the club by the hands – an action that surely has infuence on the power triangle (arm–shoulders–clubshaft moving as one unit), and possibly introduces tension and unwanted wrist action. Also, such a manipulation has to be timed correctly and performed uniformly from swing to swing to be consistent. So, the first advantage is this: If the club is always on plane, there is no need for any corrective action in the downswing and the swing is simpler, making it easier to repeat.

2. **Plane** & simple

When you try to swing on plane right from the start of the backswing, you must rotate the left arm clockwise early to make the club stay on plane. (It has a tendency to go outside and up especially if you try to do a one-piece takeaway.) This rotation is most important in obtaining a good top of the backswing position, because it opens the club and makes room for the whiplash-effect in the downswing. Or stated differently: If you do not rotate the club open in the backswing, it can only close during the downswing leading to a hook, a block, or similar unwanted result.

3. One swing **for all shots**

When you keep the club on plane from takeaway, you can stop your swing at any time, reverse direction, and hit the ball. A half, a three quarter, and all other abbreviated swings have the same takeaway and the same motor (the body rotating into the ball). This greatly simplifies your short game and introduces a wonderful coherence between short swings and full swings, something a player with a quirky backswing can't obtain.

The best, or rather worst, example of a player with a quirky backswing is Miller Barber, who had the most interesting looped swings you can imagine. Something like a latter day Jim Furyk, only more pronounced. Obviously, when you take the club away very steeply or very flat, you need a lot of rearranging (bringing the club on plane) before you can hit the ball. The corrective motion depends on the length of the swing – having the effect that your full swing feels (and is) very different from your short swings. When swinging on plane, you play only one ball game. Your full swings are longer and may be quicker than the truncated swings, but you easily feel the familiarity, because of the identical takeaway and geometry.

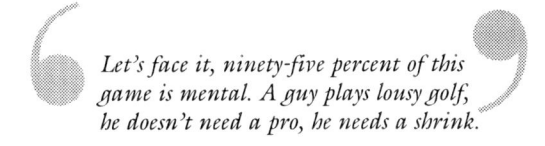

> *Let's face it, ninety-five percent of this game is mental. A guy plays lousy golf, he doesn't need a pro, he needs a shrink.*
>
> – Tom Murphy

Chapter 10

Golf swing **myths**
(Bad advice and why it can wreck your game)

Listening to, and accepting, incorrect advice is the main reason that lots of golfers have trouble improving their games. It clutters the mind with incorrect information and creates a conflict between what the golfer does and what he thinks he does or should be doing.

There is tons of advice to be found in magazines, instruction books and on the Internet, some of which is worthless and some of which is useful under specific circumstances. You will realize the limitations and the potental problems of such "instruction" by reading and understanding this work.

CHAPTER 10 | THE SCIENTIFIC TRUTH OF THE GOLF SWING

> **MYTH:** The ball should be played inside the front (left) heel.

TRUTH: **NO**, not generally, because this is a very poorly defined position. Consider two players, one using a very wide stance and the other a narrow stance. The former would play all shots with the ball far forward in the stance, positioned in front of the head, opposite the left shoulder. The latter would play the ball in the center of the stance, positioned opposite the head or the left side of the of the head as seen from the players view. Thus, this advice doesn't indicate a fixed ball position. A far better recommendation is to position the ball in relation to the golfer's head and/or shoulders, as these define the swing's center. The corresponding advice would be to position the ball opposite the golfers face for low shots that require a downward hit, and opposite the left shoulder for shots that need a high trajectory and a sweeping motion of the club.

> **MYTH:** A strong grip produces hooks – a week grip produces slices.

TRUTH: **NOT AT ALL.** Two of the greatest exponents of the faded ball flight, Lee Trevino and Jack Nicklaus, both used strong grips. As the hands are pretty passive in a swing controlled by the body, you can hit any type of shot with any grip. On top of this, it is easier to block the release of the club with your hands when using a strong grip, thus hitting a straight shot or a fade.

> **MYTH:** The left arm should be kept straight during the swing.

TRUTH: This is a killer for introducing unwanted tension in the backswing and weird, contorted positions at the top. Please remember that both arms support the club in the swing, and that very few golfers are supple and loose enough to swing with a straight left arm. It's great if you can do it, but if not, don't worry.

> **MYTH:** A wide, one-piece takeaway, will bring power to the swing.

TRUTH: **NO.** A wide, one-piece takeaway is likely to prevent the golfer from reaching a good position at the top of the backswing by introducing tension. This advice often leads to a steep position at the top, from where the golfer hits slices, blocks, and quick hooks when his timing is off. Please remember, there is no one correct way to swing back. The perfect position at the top can be reached in a large number of ways.

> **MYTH:** You need to restrain the hips from moving while turning the shoulders as much as possible.

TRUTH: **NO.** This advice introduces unwanted tension, and cuts down on the length of the swing and your leg action – unless you are extraordinarily supple. Most golfers need more leg action and more active legs in their swings, but John Daly could probably benefit from this advice as it would firm up and shorten his action, thus providing more precision. The amount of turn that is right for you depends on your build, the length of your spine, and the length of your legs. It comes naturally when you focus on turning your shoulders "with your legs."

MYTH: The coil of the backswing represent stored energy that is released during the downswing.

TRUTH: **NO WAY.** Muscles and tendons are not elastic – they won't store energy like a spring. This is a preposterous suggestion that corresponds to stating that a bent arm springs open by itself when you relax it. Your arm stays bent until you choose to straighten it through a deliberate action. (The muscles used for straightening the arm are not even the same muscles that bends it.) Likewise, the golf swing – the backswing puts your body in an alert position where some of your muscles can apply force through contraction and leverage. The key to a powerful swing is to involve as many muscles as possible and have them work over as great a distance as possible.

MYTH: You should "shift your weight" during the swing – from the front foot to the rear foot and back to the front foot.

TRUTH: This is a certain way of wrecking your swing – by separating lower body movement from upper body movement. It is true that this infamous weight shift often can be measured in good players, but it is merely a result of the player using his entire body to power the swing. Better advice is to focus on turning your body into the ball, counter-clockwise as seen by the right-handed player. If you watch video footage of Greg Norman in his prime in the 1980s, observe that he often kicks backward with his right leg during the downswing. This indicates that he is trying to turn his hips powerfully into the shot. If he tried to shift his weight, he would jump onto his toes instead.

MYTH: You should pull down with the arms during the first part of the downswing.

TRUTH: NOT IN GENERAL. This advice is only applicable when you have a very steep backswing. If you lift your hands and arms high above your shoulders when swinging back, this action can prevent you from coming over the top in the downswing.

MYTH: You should swing to the ball from the inside.

TRUTH: This poorly defined advice doesn't apply to the swing in general. The club should always travel inside a plane defined by the target line and vertical, unless the player is hitting an intentional fade or slice that starts left of target. But, the correct arm swing is, in fact, a very steep outside to inside motion with reference to the shoulders. This is why players who predominantly use their arms always slice or pull hooks.

CHAPTER 10 | THE SCIENTIFIC TRUTH OF THE GOLF SWING

MYTH: The clubhead should strike the ball from inside-to-out thus producing draw spin.

TRUTH: I am not absolutely sure that it is, in fact, possible to swing a golf club with square face from inside the target line to outside the target line – but, I know for a fact that whenever the clubhead is open or closed in relation to its path, the ball curves left and right respectively. So, it is perfectly possible to hit a hook with an out-to-in swing and a slice with an in-to-out swing. The hook starts left and moves even further left and the slice starts right and curves further right. Or, in other words, an inside-to-out path doesn't, in itself, produce draw spin.

MYTH: You should use your right hand to "whip the club through" at impact.

TRUTH: No person has the ability to time this motion consistently, which does take place in the swing, but the right hand is pulled through by the momentum of the club – it doesn't provide the energy for the motion. Many great swingers (most notably Vijay Singh) sport a right hand that is almost off the grip entirely through impact. This doesn't correspond to the right hand being the powerhouse of the swing.

> **MYTH:** The hips move less than 2 miles per hour and therefore cannot produce speed.

TRUTH: Oh dear, another gross misconception of physics (blatantly put forward by the self-appointed golf "professor" Jack Kuykendall). Try swinging a yo-yo or some other object on a string. You can make the object travel very fast, yet your hand is barely moving. But, it does provides the centripetal force that makes the object travel in a circular motion. (Centripetal means directed toward the center). A major part of a good swing is the ability to provide the centripetal force necessary to sustain the circular motion. This force is rather large and causes a player with a poor posture to loose balance.

> **MYTH:** When you hit down on the ball it goes up into the air.

TRUTH: Strictly speaking, this is not true. If you hit a shot from a down-slope, say 15 degrees, the ball starts 15 degrees lower than when hit from a level lie. Correspondingly, a ball hit from an up-slope starts higher. So, the steeper downward the clubhead travels at impact, the lower the shot. All other things being equal "hitting down" on the ball produces flatter shots!

But, "hitting down" is also, somewhat misleading, used to describe "getting to the bottom of the ball," that is, hitting the ball high on the club face. This results in a high trajectory because the club's center of gravity is below the impact point.

CHAPTER 10 | THE SCIENTIFIC TRUTH OF THE GOLF SWING

> **MYTH:** With a steep swing plane it is easier to extricate the ball from rough because the club has to travel through less grass to the ball.

TRUTH: This is a poorly defined statement that fails to take into consideration the concepts of swing plane, club lie angle, and downward hit. If a player has a very upright swing plane and is using very upright clubs, then he has a slim theoretical advantage over other players. But, there are other concepts to consider: All good players retain the release of the club until just before impact. Thus, the club always travels steeply downward, minimizing the amount of grass between club and ball. And, if the player uses clubs with standard lies, the path of the clubhead during release is virtually identical, no matter how steep the swing plane. When hitting from rough, it's far more important not to use a club with too little loft than to have a steep swing plane. But, a player with a very flat backswing has to modify his takeaway to avoid having the grass grab the club – which is not a big problem for players with steep backswings.

> **MYTH:** A drive hit with top spin will travel further – especially into the wind.

TRUTH: No correctly hit golf ball travels with top spin. If possible to hit at all, a shot with top spin won't soar, but dives straight into the ground reducing distance to an absolute minimum.

> **MYTH:** There exists many different swing methods: the classical swing, the square-to-square swing, the modern swing – and some golfers are hitters others are swingers.

TRUTH: **NO.** All **good** swings are based on identical fundamentals. The power is generated by the body turning in relation to the ground. Take Snead, Hogan, and Nelson in the 1940s, send them through a worm-hole to the present, dress them up in Lindeberg apparel, and everyone would claim that they were the stars of the future. There is nothing new under the sun – except maybe for the fashion statements.

> **MYTH:** The shaft loads during the backswing and unloads during the downswing providing extra speed to the clubhead.

TRUTH: **NO.** And, a fallacy for many reasons: The amount of energy capable of being stored in a shaft is very small compared to the total required energy; on top of this, the shaft doesn't bend backward but bends upward (toe up) during the downswing. So, if this effect were real, it would propel the clubhead into the ground, not forward.

CHAPTER 10 | THE SCIENTIFIC TRUTH OF THE GOLF SWING

> **Myth:** A draw flies further than a fade due to the hook spin.

Truth: **No.** Sound logic tells us that ball spin is invariant to left and right – draw and fade – hook and slice. It simply doesn't matter, some golfers hit their longest shots with a draw and others with a fade. But, if you hit with one given club, you'll find that the draws go lower and, thus, longer than the fades, because the effective loft of the club is reduced when hitting draws (closed face) and increased when hitting fades (open face).

> **Myth:** To hit good iron shots you need to "trap" the ball between the clubface and the ground.

Truth: **Trapping is impossible!** If the ball actually rebounded from the ground in every iron shot, the ball flight would change according to the conditions of the ground and the ball would lose a huge amount of energy. It would be impossible to hit from a high tee-peg, from rough, soft ground, sand, and other soft or irregular surfaces. So, this idea of trapping is a total fallacy. But, as a swing thought, it has some credit, because you get the best contact by hitting down and through with an iron, leading with the hands at impact. But, rebounding the ball of the turf... never.

> *His swing was made in heaven, part velvet, part silk, like a royal robe, so sweet you could pour it over ice cream.*

– Jim Murray (on Tom Weiskopf)

Chapter 11

Anatomy
of the golf swing

The following is a step-by-step description of the positions and actions that lead to a compact, powerful swing.

(1) The ball position should be decided with respect to the player's head (which is fixed in relation to his swing center), not his feet, in which case the width of the stance has to be taken into account to determine the true ball position.

(2) The body should be in an alert position at address, knees bent, legs ready to move, and the back kept straight but inclined by a rotated pelvis.

(3) The arms have to rotate clockwise (open) **as seen by the player** during the backswing. In doing so, the right elbow should achieve an angle close to 90 degrees. This is **the only required** use of the arms

CHAPTER 11 | THE SCIENTIFIC TRUTH OF THE GOLF SWING

and hands during the backswing. The movement to the top of the backswing can be credited to the *body rotation*.

④ The main motion in the backswing is "the legs turning the shoulders." You should focus on using the legs because they also start the downswing and work through to the completion of the swing. Mentally, you should concentrate on rotating your body around your spine or an axis just outside your spine.

⑤ The purpose of the backswing is solely to prepare for the forward swing. There should be very little tension (because tension does no good) and your feet/legs should remain in control at all time.

⑥ The move to start the downswing and, in fact, the only move toward the ball, should be a turning of the body counter-clockwise. This is the main power move of the swing and it should be kept up until your chest faces the target.

⑦ The shoulders should not be unwound consciously in the downswing. The swing thought should be to keep the relative position of shoulders and hips intact.

⑧ The arms should also be kept in their top of the backswing position, with the right elbow bent long into the forward swing. This is one of the real "secrets" in golf; the arms are operating totally opposite to what many instructors and players preach: The player moves the club toward the ball by rotating his body into the ball – not by releasing the club with his hands toward it. The centrifugal force acting on the clubhead tries to make the club release when the rotation speeds up.

(9) As the downswing starts with a rotation initiated by the legs, the club and arms come down in the forward swing on a steep angle – a potential over-the-top motion. This is why it is best to be on-plane at the top of the backswing. Then, the downswing is steep but not outside the line. If you start the downswing from a very upright position (with the arms lifted high above the shoulders), you introduce an extra parameter (the downward movement of the arms) and you need a precise synchronization between the rotating body and the arm swing. This, I believe, is what Faldo and Leadbetter worked on eliminating during Faldo's successful revamping of his swing in the early 1990s.

(10) As you turn into the ball, you find yourself in the infamous late-hit position where the inertial forces from the rotation release the club toward the ball.

(11) Checkpoints (at impact):
- Hands in front of ball
  Indicates that the clubhead hasn't overtaken the hands. Provides best ball flight. Advice works for every club in the bag, including the putter.
- Left shoulder high and in front of the ball
  Indicates that the body has produced power, that the left arm hasn't broken down, and that the clubhead hasn't passed the hands.
- Spine vertical or tilted away from target
  Indicates that the swing correctly is directed forward – not downward.
- Hips facing target
  (and turned much more than shoulders)
  Indicates that the legs have been working (producing power) in the downswing and that the upper body has not overtaken the lower body.

- Right elbow bent
  Indicates that the arms are passive – there is no release before the ball has been hit.

(12) Not until about 4 o'clock (seen face-on by an observer) are both arms straight and the club fully released. The club shaft is still on-plane and pointing to the right of the target but the clubface is closed and points down toward the ground.

(13) The left arm should bend early in the follow-through. It is of no benefit to keep it straight for as long as possible – this hinders a good release. Both arms swing very much to the inside in the follow-through of a good swing, because they follow the rotating body.

(14) Checkpoint:
The club releases powerfully due to the whiplash-effect. This can throw the lower (right) hand of the grip after impact, which is not necessarily a fault but it shows that the player has not hindered the release by holding the club too tight.

Where to go from here?

Use a scientific approach, this guide, and a video camera. Work on understanding the arm movement and the body turn. Experiment, but make sure that you have a plan. Make a list of what is good and what is not. Analyze your swing and try to figure out how problematic areas are interrelated and how they can be elliminated. Write down your solutions and try them out, one by one.

Finally, be positive and have fun. You are approaching golf nirvana.

A

accelerate through the ball 18
acceleration of ball at impact 17
address
   distance from the ball 60
   position 58
   weight distribution 60
air density influence on ball flight 36
air resistance
   influence on ball flight 36
airflow around spinning golf ball 33
always ask "why"
   before you accept golf tips" 54
analogy
   hammering nails 42
   hammer throwing 64-65
   learning mathematics 6
   propeller aircraft 65
   tennis player 56
   tightrope walker 27
   tug of war 68
anatomy of the golf swing 87
angle of attack 20, 22
angular momentum is conserved
   in the golf swing 48
angular velocity 44
arm movement 55, 61, 68, 87
   exercise 69
arms
   passive 66
   rotate open in backswing 87
   true role in the swing 65
axis of rotation 64

B

backspin 20-22
   all shots have backspin 24
   tilted backspin axis 35
backswing 41
   as a fashion statement 73
   left arm rotates 76
   path 73
balancing pole 27
balata 19
ball
   aerodynamics 33
   cover 19
   position in stance 58, 78, 87
   trajectory 19, 33
ballet of man and club 11
balls optimised for
   different clubhead speeds 19
   different trajectories 19
Barber, Miller 76
benefits of swinging on plane 75-76
bent right arm at impact 89
Bernoulli effect 33
big turn 44, 63

biomechanics
   an equaliser 44
   muscles and tendons do not
   store energy 80
body
   in alert position 87
   pace of movement 68
body rotation 55, 61-63, 88
body turn 62
bulge (on clubface) 29
bunker 17, 23

C

carbon fibre 23
carry of 350 yards 40
centre of gravity 29
centre of mass of clubhead 25
centrifugal force 88
   on the clubhead 72
cetripetal force
   makes an object travel in a curve 83
Characteristic Time [CT] 20
characteristics of a good grip 57
checkpoints at impact 89-90
closed stance 49
closed vs. open notation
   has general validity 4, 47
club
   design 25
   heavy 23
   immune to bad hits 24
   release 47
clubface
   open & closed (definitions) 50
   opening in the backswing 50
   orientation 35, 50
   orientation relative to
   swing path 50
   square (definition) 50
clubhead
   centre of mass 25
   heavy needs stiffer shaft 31
   mass versus ball speed 23
   shape 25
   speed 150 mph 40
   speed required for
   long iron shots 38
   sweet spot 25
   twisting at impact 26
collision 19
coming over the top 70, 89
COR, coefficient of restitution 19-20
counteracting the effect of wind 37
cover of ball 19
cupping the left wrist 71
curving shots are difficult to avoid 35

D
Daly, John 52, 79
data for impact
   5-iron 21
   driver 21
   wedge 21
David Leadbetter's set-up routine 55
distance
   chart 39
   from the ball 60
   of golf shots 37
divot 16
downswing 41
   how to start 67
draw 35, 82
   how to set up for a draw 49
   driver 20
   distance in carry 39
drives with top spin 84
Duval, David 67

E
effect of clubhead mass
   on ball speed 23
effective loft 21
elastic collision 19
energy 43, 65
   kinetic 44
   lost at impact 19
   stored energy myth 80
   passive transmission 65
   from club to ball 17, 21
explosion shots 17

F
face curvature 29
fade 35, 82
   how to set up for a fade 49
fairway bunker shot 23
fairway metal 29
fairway wood 17, 20
Faldo, Nick 68, 89
fast acceleration makes up
   for short swing path 42
fat strike 14, 16
feedback felt by the hands 23
   uncomfortable 26
female golfers 3
first move from the
   top-of-backswing position 88
flat swing 52
flat swings look short 52
flexibility of golfer's body 43
flyer 22
force
   centripetal 83
   muscular 43
   of gravity 42
   of impact 18, 20

forces on the shaft 32
friction, clubface and ball 22-23
full swing vs. truncated swing 39
fundamentals found in all swings 3, 85
Furyk, Jim 76
game improving clubs 26
gap wedge 39

G
Garcia, Sergio 71
Garner, John 41
gear-effect 29
golf ball 18-19
Golf Channel 7
Golf Digest 39, 40, 66
golf
   is a serial game 10
   nirvana 4, 90
   rules 19
golf swing
   good 9
   perfect 8
golfer
   female 3
   handicap player 38
   left-handed 3
   professional player 38
   strong 44
golfing gorillas 40
good golf swing 9
gravity 42
Greg Norman's backward kick 81
grip strength 44
grip twisting at impact 26

H
half swing 39
hammer analogy 42
hammer throwing analogy 64-65
hands and arms player 47
hands and shoulders
   overuse of 12
head kept still 67
heavy versus light clubs 23
height of shots 34
high hands 70
   exercise 70
high tech materials 23
hip turn 62
hips facing target at impact 89
hitting down 15
hitting versus swinging 44, 85
Hogan, Ben 16, 51-52, 71, 85
hook 35, 82
   quick hook 35
how to hit
   draws and fades 50
   from grass 15
how we learn golf 12

I
impact 17, 22
   acceleration of ball 17
   clubhead speed at impact 18
   force 18, 20
   velocity of ball 17
   velocity of club 17
impact vs. address positions 22
importance of being earnest 37
improve with
   scientific approach 90
initial conditions
   determine the ball flight 33
initial velocity 22
inside-to-out swing myth 82
Internet instruction 7
iron 14, 20
   perimeter weighted 26
   Ping 27
irons
   distance chart 37
   short irons hit straight 38
   trapping 86

J
Jones, Bobby 64, 73

K
kinetic energy 44
Kuehne, Hank 66
Kuykendall, Jack 83

L
lack of understanding
   of fundamental physics 41
lag is essential in the swing 44
late hit 16, 71, 89
launch angle 24
   keep low into strong wind 36
Leadbetter, David 55, 56, 89
learning process for adults 12
left arm
   bent in follow-through 90
   kept straight during the swing 79
left arm rotation in the backswing 75
left hand grip characteristics 57
left heel 64
left-handed golfers 3
   look different 4
Leonard, Justin 39
letting shots ride the wind 37
lift on ball 34
   negative 24
Lindeberg apparel 85
lob wedge 39, 40
loft 20
   effective 21
   negative 24
   positive 24

long swing path makes up
   for slow acceleration 44
longdriving 40
long hitters
   what to learn from photos 66
looping the swing 76
lorythmic scale 28
low swing speed equals
   small forces in the swing 30
main cause of slice
   is a faulty backswing 71

M
mannerisms
   seen in good players 3, 8
margin for error
   hitting the ball 14
   hitting the target 35
mass of an object 27
measuring swing-weight 28
metal wood 29
Michelson, Phil 39
mishit 14, 26
misinformation 5, 12
missing link of golf 6
modern swing 74
MOI moment of inertia 27, 29
   club 28
   clubhead 28
muscles and tendons
   do not store energy 80
muscular action 18
muscular force 44
myths 12, 30, 77-86
   a steep swing plane is better
      from rough 84
   accelerate through the ball 18
   drives hit with top spin travels further 84
   hit down to get the ball in the air 84
   hook spin gives more distance 86
   inside-to-out produces a draw 82
   swing from the inside 81
   the hands whip the club
      through at impact 81
   the shaft is the engine
      of the swing 85
   you need to trap the ball
      when hitting irons 86

N
Nelson, Byron 85
newton, unit of force [N] 18
Newton's apple 42
Nicklaus, Jack 70, 71
Norman, Greg 81
Norman, Moe 74
notations 47

O

O'Connor Snr, Christy 19
off-center hit 29
one-piece takeaway 74
on plane swing 75
open stance 49
opening of the clubface
 in the backswing 50
optical illusion
 distorts the way
  we perceive heights 34
 shows unreal shaft flex 31
ounce-inches 28
out of bounds [OB] 10

P

pace of the body movement 68
perfect swing 66
perimeter weighing 26, 29
physical strength is not that
 important for good golf 12
physics, a fundamental lack of
 understanding 41
Ping - the company 26
Ping irons 27
play smart and score low 38
playing professionals 11
playing safe 10
power source of the swing 47
preventing the club from releasing 72
professional golfers
 a long hitting bunch 38
propeller aircraft analogy 65
pulling down with the arms
 from the top 81
purpose of the backswing 88

Q

quick hook 35
quitting on the shot 18, 68

R

reach for the sky 70
release of club 90
 happens automatically 47
 is complete after impact 66
reverse-C position 74
right hand comes off the grip 82, 90
right hand grip 58, 72
role of
 the hands 57
 the legs 66-69
Royal and Ancient Golf Club of
 St. Andrews [R&A] 19
rotation axis for the body 64
rough, hitting from 16

S

safe play 10
sand iron 39
Scott, Adam 39
scramble (match form) 9
sculled shot 16
Search for the Perfect Golf Swing
 (book) 3
serial game 10
set up in an alert posture 56
set-up geometry 58
shaft 30
 dynamic forces 32
 flexible 31
 loaded during the swing 30
 mass 30
 perfect 31
 stiffness 30
 strained during the swing 30
 torsional stiffness 31
Shepard, Alan 42
shot
 curving 35
 explosion 17
shoulders, arms and hands
 rotate as one unit 72
sidespin on ball 35, 50
Singh, Vijay 39, 82
slice 35, 82
Snead, Sam 67, 68, 85
software for golf analysis 22
sole-plate 29
Solheim, Karsten 26
Sörenstam, Annika 67
speed
 of clubhead 19, 23, 40
 required for long iron shots 38
spine angle 89
spine position at address 59
springiness
 of ball 19
 of clubface 20
spring-like effect 20
stance
 square 48
 closed 49
 opened 49
starting down from the top 88
steep swing plane 70, 74
 better from rough myth 84
stored energy myth 80
straight left arm 79
Strata (ball brand) 19
strike
 effortless 25
 less than perfect 36
 perfect 25
stroke and distance penalty 10
strong golfer 44
strong grip myth 78
superimposing arm movement

on the body turn 70
sweet spot 25
swing
    from the inside 81
    objective 13
    path 48, 49
    perfect 66
    wristy 44
swing plane (definition) 51
    as a frame of reference 52
swing thought 18, 86
    keep position of shoulders
        and hips intact 88
    legs turning the shoulders 88
swinging on plane 74-76
swinging versus hitting 44
swing-weight 28
    how to measure 28
    lorythmic scale 28

T
taking a turf 16
target line 48, 49
tennis player analogy 56
tension 44
    doesn't equal power 63
    unwanted 79
test the solidity of your grip 57
The Modern Fundamentals of Golf
    (book) 52
thin strike 14
three quarter swing 39
titanium 23
top spin on a golf ball is a fallacy 84
Top-Flite (brand name) 19
topped shot 21
torque
    from a bad hit 25
    from club's weight 28
    from impact 26
torsion stiffness of shaft 31
transfer of energy
    from club to ball 17
trapping the irons 86
Trevino, Lee 19
true role of the arms 65, 88
tug of war analogy 68
turn, big 44
two primary movements 61
two-lever system 44

U
United States Golf Association
    [USGA] 19
unwanted tension 79
use a video camera
    to record your swing 75

V
velocity
    angular 44
    initial 22
    of ball 17
    of club 17, 20
video camera 7
    record your swing 75, 90
    use to check dynamic lie angle 22

W
websites
    specialising in golf instruction 7
wedge distance chart 39
weight shift 67, 80
what is
    a fundamentally sound swing 3
whiplash-effect 44, 90
why to avoid a wide,
    one piece takeaway 79
width of stance 58
Wie, Michelle 66
wind influence
    on ball flight 36
    on club selection 36
    how to play in wind 36
Wolter, Carl 40
woods (clubs) 14, 17, 20, 29
    distances 29
Woods, Tiger 39
work done by aircraft propeller 65
worm-killer (topped shot) 24
wrist action
    should be passive 47
wrist cupping for a late hit 71
wristy swing 44

Y
yo-yo
    centripetal force 83

95

Printed in the United Kingdom
by Lightning Source UK Ltd.
123780UK00002B/305/A